A Time to Remember

TEACHINGS

Edited by Barry L. Callen

Church of God Heritage Series

**Published by
Warner Press, Inc.
Anderson, Indiana**

Publisher's Note: This is the third volume in a series of six books edited by Dr. Callen. For the sake of indexing the entire series, we show the series page numbers in parentheses beside the regular volume page numbers.

Copyright © 1978 by Warner Press, Inc.
All rights reserved.
Printed in the United States of America
ISBN 0-87162-205-X

TABLE OF ENTRIES

Characteristic Doctrinal Emphases

iv

CHRISTIAN UNITY AND WORLD PEACE

INTRODUCTION

THE EARLY leaders of the Church of God reformation movement judged aspects of the life of the Christian community previously known to them to have been infiltrated with errors and abuses of divine truth. These wrongs cried out for correction. Although often not by direct design and usually with much inconvenience to themselves, these sensitive Christians began moving into the spiritual vacuum.

Whatever the special emphases they made and prominent problems they addressed, however, it is a fact of major importance that a basic characteristic of the teachings of this new movement was the conscious rejection of the temptation to be *innovators* in either Christian doctrine or practice. To the contrary, they were calling for a fresh commitment to the foundational beliefs and practices inspired by God, recorded in the Bible, and interpreted by the Holy Spirit. They developed a conviction that their divine commission was nothing short of representing and encouraging on a worldwide scale the modern restoration of apostolic faith, practice, fellowship, and mission. Their longing was to return to the original essence of Christianity, casting aside the tangle of churchly debris that had accumulated over the centuries because of the faithlessness and ignorance, and even pride and selfishness, of many Christian churchmen. To what Christ had defined and commanded they would be true. To that they would add nothing; from that they would drop nothing. And for this cause they would give their all!

It was judged that attempts to standardize Christian truth in formal and final definitions would to some degree bind the work of the Holy Spirit, retard the emerging of the fuller truth, and artificially stagnate the life of the Church. It was believed that God has and will continue to take the initiative in making his truth known. No organizational pattern or restrictive creedal statement, no human desire or activity should be tolerated if its impact is to impede the free flow of

God's creating and organizing and commissioning of his own Church. In short, Daniel S. Warner, a prominent early leader, consistently maintained that he had "simply discovered one great spiritual principle, which was the identification of the visible and invisible church in a spiritual congregation of Christians from which no Christian was excluded by any man-made rules or corporate forms of organization."

When considering the teachings of this movement across a century of time, we encounter a subtle, central, and probably inevitable paradox. On the one hand, the movement has always been very conscious of and committed to biblical truth. Doctrinal preaching and writing have been respected highly and a concern for theological correctness has been apparent in local situations. From almost the beginning this movement has evolved a rather well-defined and generally understood *consensus of thought* concerning the basic outline of what has been conceived as constituting accurate and acceptable and minimal Christian teaching. This general focusing of opinion, shifting slightly at points over the years and never quite formalized, undoubtedly has helped to give a relatively small and (by usual standards) quite unstructured group of Christians the corporate identity and cohesiveness needed for them to relate meaningfully and to work fruitfully together.

On the other hand, a central part of this traditional theological consensus has been a persistent opposition to the tyranny of theological creeds and to the development by the movement of its own "denominational" characteristics. There has been a *holistic* emphasis, a vision of all of God's people, a reaching toward all of the truth, knowing always that no one person or creedal statement (limited as they are and well-intentioned as they might be) will ever be in a position to become the final authority. The only recognized boundary of the Christian fellowship has been the experience of salvation.

Thus the paradox. Participants in the Church of God reformation movement have functioned together with a rather clear set of goals and (for the most part) with basic theological agreement, while at the same time they have been committed in principle to being above all of the narrowing effects of denominationalism. Living with this paradox has been judged hypocritical by some Christians who continue to see denominationalism as unavoidable and even desirable. They have seen the movement's consensus of thought as clearly denominational in character. Other Christians have studied the movement's vision and life and have used words like *admirable* and *idealistic* and have judged it to be most commendable, despite its inevitable destiny of frustration.

But whatever criticisms others may have, the movement knows itself to have caught a glimpse of what God intends for his people. Thus motivated, it has called for the emergence of Christian persons who are deeply committed to Christ, who have been genuinely changed by the Spirit, who are hungering daily for a further maturing of their spiritual experience and understanding, who have been seized by a vision of all of God's people as one united and loving family, and who are humble and tolerant enough to keep growing and learning without restricting the freedom of others to do the same. The Church is known as nothing less than the fellowship of all blood-washed persons. It is entered not by the meeting of any set of human regulations, but by the action of God in granting spiritual rebirth. It operates primarily by God's gifting of his children for their individual ministries within the whole body of the Church in an orchestrated manner that will be a witness to all the world.

A vision of the Church that is this divinely oriented, that is by intent inclusive of all Christians, that is so open to more of the truth, that refuses to recognize human standards and organizations as legitimate fences that should divide Christians from each other, does indeed demand admiration. It also has made this visionary movement unusually vulnerable to criticism when the movement's own functioning has proven at any point to be something less than the ideal for which it stands. Still, this vision is vigorously maintained because it continues to commend itself as God's will for his people.

The ranks of the Church of God reformation movement have been populated over the years largely by Christians with a perpetual youth about them. Their desire has been to adventure with Christ and with each other after the very horizons of spiritual experience and understanding. Uniformity has not always been present among them and experimentalism often has been adopted as a friend. Generally speaking, diversity and flexibility have been welcomed so long as the former has remained firmly committed to Christ and the latter has been an honest attempt to adapt methods for the sake of effective Christian mission in a changing world.

It has been a difficult task to select from the entire body of literature of this movement those pieces which best represent the thrust and range of its teachings. Although no one book or author can be said to present the "official" teachings, the selections that follow, when taken together, are representative of the basic consensus of thought on central issues, worded in various ways by widely known and respected authors and institutions from all generations of the movement's history. Again, all viewpoints expressed are not necessarily in full agreement with each other. But of course, we could hardly expect an ever-searching and maturing movement of free and individual disciples of Christ in many lands across a century of time to always have played exactly the same note on the same instrument. There are many beautiful notes and a wide range of instruments in the orchestra of God's family. The crucial point is that all of these be disciplined by the same Spirit so that there should emerge among God's people a loving orchestration of heart and mind "so that the world may know."

> Barry L. Callen
> Anderson, Indiana

The Teachings
of Daniel S. Warner

A Second Work of Grace

by
Daniel S. Warner

Excerpted from a booklet entitled, "Bible Proofs of the
Second Work of Grace," by Harold L. Phillips (Anderson,
Ind.: Gospel Trumpet Company, n.d.). This booklet is a brief
digest of Warner's book by the same title, published in 1880.
The thoughts and wording are as faithful to the original as
revised paragraphing and sentence structure will allow.

THE CHURCH is God's appointed means of saving the
world. But perfect holiness is her normal condition. And
holiness is only attained by a definite grasp of faith, and it
cannot be thus appropriated until presented to the mind in a
definite form.

Having, therefore, a clear conviction that upon the preaching and testimony of entire sanctification as a distinct experience subsequent to justification, more than upon all else
besides, depends the salvation of immortal souls, the safety
of converts, the purity and consequent power, peace, and
prosperity of the church, and the glory of God; and perceiv-
ing that this "second grace" is the ultimate end of Christ's
death, and the great burden of the apostolic ministry, I was
constrained to dedicate forever unto the Lord all the energies
of my being for the promotion of this great salvation.

Perfection, as applied to redeemed souls, denotes the complete moral restoration of man from the effects of the Fall. Not physical or mental restoration, for that will not be until the Resurrection. And as the fall of man effaced the image of God from the soul and sent a current of depravity down through the entire race, the perfect restoration of the soul must, necessarily, reinstate its former purity and divine likeness.

Christian perfection is, therefore, in *kind* and not in degree. In other words, it is the perfection of our moral nature, and not the development or full growth of our powers. This position is well established in Hebrews 10:14-15: "For by one offering he [Christ] hath perfected forever them that are sanctified. Whereof the Holy Ghost also is a witness to us." The *state* of perfection, we are here told, is entered by the *work* of sanctification. And we read that Christ sanctifies "the people with his own blood" (Heb. 13:12). And the "blood of Jesus Christ his Son cleanseth us from all sin" (I John 1:7). Hence perfection is the *state* of being *free from sin*.

Surely, no one ever received the testimony of God's Spirit that he was perfect in degree, or had reached the summit of Christian growth, beyond which he could never become more wise, strong, or fruitful. But thousands have received the Spirit's witness of perfect heart purity. It is generally believed that our moral and mental powers are susceptible of endless development.

But the Bible teaches a perfection in this life that can never be improved upon: "He hath perfected forever them that are sanctified." Conybeare and Howson render as follows: "By one offering he hath perfected forever the purification of them whom he sanctifieth." Perfection, then, as attainable in this life, is confined to man's purity and what is necessarily therein included. Consistent with the Bible and universal experience it cannot be otherwise defined. While our physical and mental defects remain until the Resurrection, our moral nature alone is susceptible of perfection now, and that only in quality, leaving all the powers of the soul free to enlarge in magnitude. Being "made free from sin" and "renewed in the image of God," as first created, the soul cannot become more pure, and is therefore "perfected forever" (2 Cor. 3:18; Eph. 4:23-24; 5:26-27; Col. 3:10).

Growing into sanctification is a . . . fatal delusion. Every newborn soul, sooner or later, discovers a great want in his heart. From the day of their conversion grace had led the newborn souls to hunger and pray for and expect a better experience, a deeper work, a complete salvation from sin. But having no Joshua to lead them into the desired rest of soul, they finally conclude that they must give up seeking a better experience and become pure by growth.

Growth, in no instance, changes the nature of anything; it only increases its size, or degree; while cleansing is a process of diminishing. The first is natural and progressive, the second done at a stroke.

I hope you can see that the implanting of a new life and new nature is one thing (done at regeneration); the removal of every obstruction and antagonism to the new nature another (accomplished by the blood of Christ in entire sanctification); and that the growth of that plant is still another thing.

The whole is analogous to the implanting of seed; the removal of all noxious weeds, roots, and plants from the soil; and the growth of the plant. The first and second are *instantaneous works*, produced by an extrinsic agent; the last a gradual and natural process commenced in the first state, but greatly accelerated by the *work of purging away the old nature*, or inbred sin.

Thirteen years of experience, observation, and conversation among faithful believers in this initial grace clearly evince to me that there is an underlying sentiment, quite common, that the Bible is not altogether practical; that it is a pure and perfect standard which all should aim at, but no one can expect to measure up to in this life. This crops out in expressions as follows: "I am *striving* to do the will of God"; "I am trying to live *as near right as I can*"; "I want to obey God just as far as it is possible." These and similar expressions, very common, all betray a half-suppressed conviction that the requirements of the Bible are somewhat beyond our capacity in our present situation.

Now whether we attribute this discrepancy to the impracticability of the Bible or the incongeniality of our condition of life we impeach the goodness and wisdom of God. We either cast upon him the blasphemous reflection that he did not know the circumstances to which we are necessitated in this world, or lacked the ability to give us a religion adapted thereto. But the "more grace" solves the difficulty. It shows us that the trouble is not in the Bible, nor external surroundings, but a want of internal conformity to God and his holy law.

Now, as old and young in the merely regenerated state find it impossible or extremely difficult to measure up to this divine rule, we are forced to conclude that the Bible is not quite practical, or there is a higher state of grace that perfectly adjusts us to the yoke of Christ and makes all Christian duty easy. The latter fact is clearly established by the Word of Truth and the testimony of all who have "perfected holiness in the fear of God."

Glory to the God of all grace! When raised into this purer atmosphere, this holy mount of "full assurance," we no longer view the Sermon on the Mount and the sublime precepts of the epistles as a standard to be admired, but never realized, but as lines along which the soul moves with the utmost ease and ecstatic delight.

To deny the higher plane of Christian experience is, therefore, to contradict Christ's representation of his service and impeach the wisdom and goodness of God. To acknowledge and embrace it is to vindicate the highest and purest precepts of the Lord and to magnify his super-abounding grace that fulfills them all in us to the praise of his glory.

The Experience of Oneness
by
Daniel S. Warner

Excerpted from *The Church of God, or What the Church Is and What It Is Not*, by Daniel S. Warner (Gospel Trumpet Company, 1885).

IN CONNECTION with his prayer for oneness, the Savior prayed the Father to sanctify the disciples and all that would believe on him through their word, which includes us. "And the glory which thou gavest me I have given them; that they may be one, even as we are one: I in them, and thou in me, that they may be made perfect in one" (John 17:22-23). Sanctification, perfection, or the glory of Christ, each relates to the same experience, and this makes God's children one. "For both he that sanctifieth and they who are sanctified are all of one: for which cause he is not ashamed to call them brethren" (Heb. 2:11).

"And he gave some, apostles; and some, prophets; and some, evangelists; and some, pastors and teachers; for the perfecting of the saints, for the work of the ministry, for the edifying of the body of Christ: till we all come in the unity of the faith, and of the knowledge of the Son of God, unto a perfect man, unto the measure of the stature of the fulness of Christ" (Eph. 4:11-13).

The salvation of the Lord which qualifies us for heaven makes us one on earth. A religion of divisions will deceive the soul. The chief object of God's ministers is to "perfect the saints." And when perfected in love and holiness, they come into the "unity of the faith once delivered unto the saints." The blood of Christ not only purifies from "all sin" and "all unrighteousness," but also sweeps away all erroneous doctrines. The Comforter guides into all truth, which involves the removal of all error. It is true that cleansing from error is not as instantaneous as cleansing from sin. But the pure in heart have perfect fellowship even though all previously conceived errors have not yet disappeared. There is therefore no real cause of division but sin. Therefore to cry against sects and divisions without first being wholly sanctified and then leading people into this precious paradise of holy love is nothing but confusion mocking confusion, or Satan buffeting Satan, as the devil flogged the sons of Sceva.

All efforts of union but that of God's holiness is as pounding cold, crooked pieces of iron against each other to make them fit together. The more blows the more crooks and differences. Put them into a furnace of white heat and they will lose their cold, stiff, crooked individuality, and flow into one mass. That is God's way of uniting his people in the fire of the Holy Spirit. All tinkering up platforms of union is wasted time. Each effort only molds another sect calf for the people to worship and wrangle over. Freedom from sin knits together in love. But all merely strapped-up unions are bundles bound together to be burned.

Bible salvation is all that is needed. This obtained, both union of heart and soul and harmony in outward worship and life will follow as a result or fruit of the Spirit. When "baptized by one Spirit into one body," and made to drink in the one divine Spirit in his fulness, there will be no trouble to "worship the Father in Spirit and in truth." For "ye shall know the truth, and the truth shall make you free." On the plane of Bible holiness no outward observances are made a test, in fact nothing is made a test of fellowship. For holy men "judge not according to the appearance, but judge righteous judgment." "If we walk in the light, as he is in the light, we have fellowship one with another, and the blood of Jesus Christ his Son cleanseth us from all sin" (1 John 1:7). Fellowship is of the Spirit (Phil. 2:1) and exists where heart-purity exists. It is the conscious blending of hearts filled with the same Holy Spirit.

One may have been led into all truth; the other not. This

does not interrupt fellowship. Nevertheless it is the duty of such as "know the truth" in meekness to instruct others who do not. Ignorance of some truth does not destroy fellowship, but resisting the truth does because it forfeits salvation. We must not sanction people's errors, but if they are saved we must show our love and fellowship to them so long as we do not get the evidence that their wrong doctrines have become willful, or they have in some way lost salvation. Then fellowship ends, but love and kindness still continue in faithful efforts for their salvation. To ignore fellowship simply because of some doctrinal error is bigotry.

To know the truth is our privilege, to teach the truth, our duty. But to have fellowship with the pure and upright of heart is an involuntary and spontaneous fact. Sects are the result of carnality; nothing but perfect holiness destroys carnality and thus removes both sectism and its cause. The fire of God's love saves the soul, harmonizes all hearts that receive it, leads them into perfect and uniform obedience to all truth, and drives afar all who refuse to pass through its purging fire and gain the plan of holy fellowship.

Our Duty Is Plain
by
Daniel S. Warner

Excerpted from *Bible Proofs of the Second Work of Grace*, by Daniel S. Warner (Goshen, Ind.: E. U. Mennonite Publishing Society, 1880).

A REVIVAL of holiness in a community is the result of personal consecration and faith; and its relapse will be in proportion to the number of individuals that remove the sacrifice from the sanctifying altar. There is no such thing as thorough holiness, except as wrought by the Sanctifier in individual hearts; and if, as I verily believe, thorough and widespread holiness destroys denominations—burns up sectarian distinctions—it must do it in your heart, as an individual. And if this work is done, the fruits must exhibit the fact; you will be "saved by the precious blood of Christ from all vain conversation, received by tradition from your fathers"; such as "your church," "our church," "our preacher opened the doors of the church," "what branch of the church do you belong to?" "You ought to join some branch."

"And if there be any other thing that is contrary to sound doctrine" (1 Tim. 1:10), that grew out of a "perversion of the right ways of the Lord" and "the gospel of Christ" (Acts 13:10, and Gal. 1:7). If the bitter root of sectism is entirely destroyed out of your heart, you will ignore all sectional lines and party fences, the dreadful curse. If you are a true, intelligent Bible Christian, a holy, God-fearing man, you must cast off every human yoke, withdraw fellowship from, and renounce every schismatic and humanly constituted party in the professed body of Christ. Instead of belonging to "some branch," you will simply belong to Christ, and be a branch yourself in him, the "true vine." Instead of remaining identified with any sect,—*i.e.,* cut-off party, directly or indirectly the results of sin—you will claim membership in, and fellowship with, the one and indivisible Church that God has on earth and which is made up of all who are born of the Spirit. On this broad and divinely established platform, and here only, can you stand clear of the sin of sectarianism and the blood of immortal souls that perish through its pernicious influence. Are you strictly loyal to God while you persist in adhering to a sect, notwithstanding he says "there should be no schism—sects—in the body." (1 Cor. 12:25)?

I am not advocating the no-church theory, but the one holy Church of the Bible, not bound together by rigid articles of faith, but perfectly united in love under the primitive glory of the Sanctifier, "continuing steadfastly in the Apostle's doctrine and fellowship," and taking captive the world for Jesus.

But it is thought that we should not fight against sects nor attempt to abolish the evil at present lest we thereby form another sect. This is virtually saying that we should "go on sinning, lest a worse thing come upon us."

An attempt to rally Israel under any of the many party-names and creeds might indeed result in a new sect. But this is not what we contend for. Nay, but let us rather burn to ashes these high places of Israel's corruption and, returning to Jerusalem, let us build upon the foundation of the Apostles and Prophets, Jesus Christ himself being the chief corner-stone. Let us abandon the nonsense of ecclesiastical succession and cease to inflate our pride and vanity by parading the good and long-since departed who innocently wore our party badges. The piety of our fathers will not atone for the worldiness of the Church at present. Let us also quit flourishing our church creeds as though their excellency were an essential supplement to the widom of inspiration. Let us, we pray you, in the name of Jesus Christ, for the sake of our holy and Divine religion and a world that is lost in sin, O let us put away these childish things and return to Jerusalem, not to form a new sect, but as the "servants of the God of Heaven and earth [let us] build the house that was builded these many years ago, which a great King of Israel [Jesus Christ] builded and set up" (Ezra 5:11).

Many say we need more union of hearts, but think a visible organic union unnecessary. But remember that it was a visible union that Jesus prayed for, such as the world could see and be thereby convinced and saved.

From what has been said and the uniform teaching of the Bible, the following facts are very evident:

1. The division of the Church into sects is one of Satan's most effectual, if not the very greatest means of destroying human souls.

2. Its enormous sin must be answered for by individual adherents to, and supporters of sects.

3. The only remedy for this dreadful plague is thorough sanctification, and this is only wrought by a personal, individual contact with the blood of Christ through faith.

4. The union required by the Word of God is both a spiritual and visible union.

5. The divisions of the Church are caused by elements that are foreign to it by deposits of the enemy, which exist in the hearts and practices of individual members, involving their responsibility and requiring their personal purgation.

These facts make *your duty* plain. What you and I want, dear reader, is "thorough and widespread holiness" in our individual souls to destroy denominationalism there. Holiness, ever so thorough and widespread around you, will not cleanse your hearts. Neither can the sin of division in the hearts and lives of others attach to you unless you drink in their spirit and also become a partisan. You need not waste time in planning general union movements or praying the Lord to restore the unity of his Church until you go down under the blood and have every bone of contention and cause of division purged out of your own heart. Then you may do something to influence others to do the same.

An Exclusive Christ
by
Daniel S. Warner

Excerpted from the tract by this title, published by the Gospel Trumpet Company (n.d.).

JESUS is the King eternal over all heaven and earth; yes, throughout the vast universe. His kingdom therefore is an exclusive kingdom. It leaves no place for any other. It is the stone that breaks all other powers to pieces, and fills the whole earth. His church is likewise exclusive; it does not "live and let live" other institutions called churches. The word of truth acknowledges no other church but the one divine fold founded by the Savior. He who discerns the sacred body of Christ is bound to discard everything else; and he who acknowledges the confused multitudes of men's creeds, and party organisms, as churches, has never "discerned the body of Christ," which is the church (Eph. 1:22-23; Col. 1:18, 24).

The Spirit of the God of the Bible is an exclusive Spirit. It repels and rejects every other spirit. God's children have all been "by one Spirit . . . baptized into one body, . . . and have been all made to drink into one Spirit" (1 Corinthians 12:13). This all-searching and eternal Spirit in the hearts of the redeemed of the Lord takes cognizance of what kind of spirits dwell in the hearts and bodies of others who claim to be the worshipers of God. If of opposite character, there is no fellowship. If all are in possession of the pure and gentle Spirit and nature of God, the blessed elements of heaven, their hearts flow joyfully together; and this is fellowship, pure, heavenly, and the source of much happiness.

To confess any religion and creed but the New Testament is to deny Christ. To confess that there is any church but the one Jesus built is to make God a liar. To be honest in the sight of God and to stand upon the offensive foundation of the exclusive Christ and his exclusive church, kingdom, and religion, is what stirs hell today, and calls out what little persecution saints have to endure in these last days.

The sects would have no objection to us accepting the Bible name, *saints,* if we would confess that they in all their pride, tobacco filth, and abominable worldly conformity, are saints also. They would not care if we do use the title given by the mouth of the Lord, viz., "the church of the living God," if we would only confess that all the sects are likewise churches of God—sister churches. But this would be confessing a falsehood. The Lord owns no sisterhood of sects. The Bible gives no place for a plurality of brotherhoods in Christ. But one is your Father, and all ye are brethren, one family in heaven and earth.

In the last few years God has raised up a people who fully discern the body of Christ. They have taken their stand upon the platform of "all truth," as it is in Christ Jesus. By the process of salvation they have been taken into the one fold of Christ (John 10:9). The Lord himself added them to his own body, the church (Acts 2:47). They teach and accept no other condition of membership in the church, than those conditions found in the Word of God. And by a life of perfect obedience to the divine will, of faith toward, and holiness unto the Lord, they have this witness that they please God, and are abiding in the one and only church of God, which is the body of Christ, and which includes all the saved in heaven and earth. They with perfect consistency and loyalty to God, reject every other so-called church but that which Christ built upon the rock; and say to all honest disciples of Christ who have been falsely taught, and taken by men into men's churches, "Come out of her," "Come out from among them." And though this is the point of offense and persecutions, by the grace of God we will not compromise the truth to save our lives.

Our Church Musicians

by
W. Dale Oldham

This article is condensed from a presentation made in Warner Auditorium at Anderson on June 13, 1976.

TONIGHT let's give special thanks to the Lord for our church musicians, both present and past. Let's thank God for Bill Gaither, whose inspired compositions so warm our hearts and thrill our souls—songs like "The Church Triumphant" and "It Will Be Worth It All." Fifty years from tonight some of you younger folk will probably say to your grandchildren and great-grandchildren, "Sure—I knew Bill personally. We used to drive a hundred miles to hear Gloria, Danny, and Bill in concert; and we always came away blessed."

But eighty years ago the bright, young, curly-haired smiling composer that all the people were talking about was Barney Warren, a tenor. He became our most prolific poet and composer. During his lifetime he furnished the church with more than 7,000 gospel songs. Generally he was responsible for both the words and the music, but he also collaborated extensively with D. S. Warner, C. W. Naylor, and others in using their song poems. He and a small group of other singers accompanying D. S. Warner in his various evangelistic meetings sang with heart-warming inspiration as they rode along in a horse-drawn wagon to the appointed place of meeting (which might be a little crossroads church, or schoolhouse, or even a brush arbor). There they sang again, with vigor and inspiration, songs that Barney had composed—and more often than not, they sang in communities unfriendly toward the truth.

Older brethren used to tell me about their singing, for they sang new songs with a new spirit. And it was their inspired music which had so much to do with bringing to birth a new spirit of reformation among the people. Inspired singers, through whom the Holy Spirit was mightily poured out upon one community after another, drew men, women, young people and children to the meetings, just as steel is drawn to a magnet.

It was inspired music, coupled to inspired preaching and witnessing, which led people to Christ and guided them into the ways of truth and righteousness. This combination led the church to become missionary-minded, evangelistically oriented. It was inspired music which challenged unbelievers until they became contrite, penitent believers, and thus members of the New Testament church. It was, to a great degree, the attractive appeal of the music which caused whatever evangelistic series was being conducted to become table conversation in hundreds of homes.

Before too long now we will be able to say, "Seventy years ago B. E. Warren wrote both the words and music to a simple gospel song titled 'A Child of God.' " Simple? Of course it's simple! But the song has movement, is easy to sing, easy to harmonize, and says what every true Christian enjoys saying by way of witness and testimony.

Go back in your imagination and see Barney Warren and his companions as they rode along on their way to the evening service, singing lustily, accompanied not by a fine symphony orchestra but by the creaking of wagon wheels and the clop, clop, clop of horses' hooves.

The words and music for "The Kingdom of Peace" were

written by B. E. Warren. I don't consider it to be one of his
better compositions, yet it proclaims a theme which was
quite popular when it was written. Our preachers used to
expound at length on the subject of a spiritual kingdom, a
kingdom not of this world, a kingdom which is indeed
"righteousness, peace, and joy in the Holy Ghost" (Rom.
14:17).

B. E. Warren knew times of great inspiration and exulta-
tion. He was no stranger, up there on Cloud Nine! His was
the soul of a poet, which means, of course, that he sometimes experienced moments of depression as well as hours
of overflowing joy and delight. In other words, B. E. Warren was a human being.

When I think of Brother Warren, I see him crossing a
campground, clipboard under his arm, stopping again and
again to visit with old friends. With some of them he had
suffered privation and persecution as they struggled to establish new churches in needy areas. That clipboard was a
part of his dress, and really should have been buried with
him. Many a time, as a sermon was going forth, Brother
Warren would be caught up with an idea for a song, and that
would be the last he heard of the message. When the service
was over, he would have a new song poem to which he
would set music at his further convenience.

"I'm Redeemed" is a song in which words and music are
by another of our pioneer ministers—J. C. Fisher, who
edited our our first song book, *Songs of Victory*, was contemporary with D. S. Warner and the two collaborated in
producing several good songs. Warner wrote the words,
Fisher the music. "I'm Redeemed" is a happy song.
You hear rejoicing in it. Our people sang a great many
similar songs during the early years of our work. That is one
reason why their religion was so contagious—it was so full
of enthusiasm and joy. "I'm Redeemed" is a positive testimony to the transforming power of the gospel. It radiates
new life and freedom from guilt and it proclaims our inde-
structible hope of eternal life. Here again is an example of a
quite ordinary song which has stayed with us for a long,

long time, simply because it sings our testimony. It makes you want to put your hand up in witness when you sing, "I'm redeemed, praise the Lord!" It declares, "I am saved from all sin, and I'm walking in the light, I'm redeemed by the blood of the Lamb."

Another of our ranking composers was D. O. Teasley. He was one of the most talented of our leaders during the first decade or two of this century. He could manage production in our publishing plant, write books of an instructive nature, sing well, direct singing, and function as a capable preacher. He was a student of harmony and composition and also a successful teacher of those subjects.

Teasley had strong confidence in the wisdom of C. W. Naylor as a competent judge of poetry, and generally he took a sheaf of his gospel songs to Naylor before permitting any of them to be published. I well remember a cold winter night early in 1921 when a quartet of us went to the Naylor home to sing the new songs Teasley had written. Among them was the selection, "We'll Praise the Lord for Sins Forgiven," now sung widely by the church. So while remembering B. E. Warren and J. C. Fisher, let us also thank God for D. O. Teasley, the tall, bass-voiced, many-talented man.

We've saved one of our best songs for the last—"The Church's Jubilee." You know, our ancestors did a considerable amount of doctrinal preaching with music. In my opinion none of the songs about the New Testament church has a greater "lift" than the one titled "The Church's Jubilee." Here we have C. W. Naylor writing the words, A. L. Byers, the music. I was Brother Naylor's pastor the last four or five years of his life and we had some interesting conversations. He saw the New Testament church not as a denomination, but as the family of God, the family of the redeemed, composed of all the saved both in heaven and earth—and none but the saved. Naylor was the one who wrote the song about heaven, which declares, "Sin Can Never Enter There."

A. L. Byers was a model of introvertive dignity. He

never talked just to pass the time. The father of five children, he built his own two-story home out of concrete blocks, manufactured right on his lot. He owned a fair-sized library of hymnals and books on composition and harmony, and loaned them out with a degree of reluctance. His music manuscripts were models of neatness and exactness. He was precise at every step of his musical composition. Every chord had to make its proper progression, its proper resolution. No consecutive fifths and octaves in Byers' music! Such a methodical and painstaking composer might have been expected to produce stilted music. The fact that he did not can be explained only by Brother Byers' love for the Lord, the church, and the truth.

As we review the work of our song writers during the early years we must be impressed by the breadth, depth, and variety of their work. Their instruments had more than one string. Some of their songs were muted, while others had a lilt and now and then were even exhuberant. Like an intelligent pastor who finds just the right diet for every sheep in his flock, our song writers eventually met the needs of every person in the congregation.

But time marches on relentlessly, and one by one the creative folk who were used so blessedly in the church in the early days as poets and composers stepped off the stage of action as they were called into the eternal presence by the One whose redemptive love had inspired this praise.

On another shore they await our coming—D. S. Warner, J. C. Fisher, B. E. Warren, C. W. Naylor, A. L. Byers, D. O. Teasley, and many, many others. Though dead, they still speak, and if they are conscious in their present state, may the inspiration with which today's church sings their songs make even more joyous and contented their immortality. For remember, we owe them a debt which can never be fully paid except through melodious praise.

I'm Redeemed

by
Joseph C. Fisher (1884)

Quoted from the *Hymnal of the Church of God*, Copyright
© 1971 by Warner Press, Inc.

I'm redeemed, I'm redeemed, from the darkness of the
night
    That so thickly enveloped my soul;
In my heart there have gleamed rays of wonderful light,
    Where the waves of thy glory now roll.

I'm redeemed by thy blood, from the power of the grave,
    And the vict'ry I have over death;
O that wonderful flood! How I felt its pow'r to save,
    When I plunged in its fathomless depth!

I'm redeemed from all sin and I'm walking in the light,
    And thy Spirit illumines my way;
I've no fear now within 'for the terror of the night,
    Nor the arrow that flieth by day.'

The redeemed ones shall walk in the pathway of the just,
    Which shines brighter and brighter each day;
They shall sing and shall talk with the bright angelic host,
    Where all sorrows and sighs flee away.

Refrain

I'm redeemed, praise the Lord!
    I'm redeemed by the blood of the Lamb;
I am saved from all sin, and I'm walking in the light,
    I'm redeemed by the blood of the Lamb.

The Bond of Perfectness
by
Daniel S. Warner (1893)

Quoted from the *Hymnal of the Church of God*, Copyright
© 1971 by Warner Press, Inc.

How sweet this bond of perfectness,
   The wondrous love of Jesus!
A pure foretaste of heaven's bliss,
   O fellowship so precious!

O praise the Lord for love divine
   That binds us all together!
A thousand chords our hearts entwine
   Forever and forever.

"God over all and in us all,"
   and thro' each holy brother;
No pow'r of earth or hell, withal,
   Can rend us from each other.

O mystery of heaven's peace!
   O bond of heaven's union!
Our souls in fellowship embrace,
   And live in sweet communion.

Refrain
O brethren, how this perfect love
   Unites us all in Jesus!
One heart, and soul, and mind we prove
   The union heaven gave us.

The Biblical Trace of the Church

by
William G. Schell (ca. 1895)

The church of the morning bright,
Like crystal so clear her light,
   Triumphant she knew no fears;
In finest white linen dressed;
Pure holiness she possessed,
   Two hundred and sev'nty years.

The sun went down ere his time,
The moon also ceased to shine,
   Left Zion in bitter tears;
No star then appeared in sight,
Oh, long, dreary Papal night!
   Twelve hundred and sixty years.

Arising the sun of day,
Disperses the night away,
   While popery quakes with fears;
Shone dimly the gospel ray,
There followed a cloudy day;—
   Three hundred and fifty years.

We welcome the evening light;
The gospel so clear and bright
   Breaks forth as in days of yore;
The mists are all cleared away,
All hail the supernal day!
   The sun shall go down no more.

Chorus

Hell never can destroy the church,
   Built by the Savior's hands;
Upon the Rock, the solid Rock,
   Christ Jesus, still she stands.

The Evening Light

by
Daniel S. Warner (1897)

Quoted from *Songs of the Evening Light* (Moundsville, W.Va.: Gospel Trumpet Publishing Company, 1897).

Brighter days are sweetly dawning,
  Oh, the glory looms in sight!
For the cloudy day is waning,
  And the ev'ning shall be light.

Misty fogs, so long concealing,
  All the hills of mingled night,
Vanish, all their sin revealing,
  For the ev'ning shall be light.

Lo! the ransomed are returning,
  Robed in shining crystal white,
Leaping, shouting home to Zion,
  Happy in the ev'ning light.

Free from Babel, in the Spirit,
  Free to worship God aright,
Joy and gladness we're receiving,
  Oh, how sweet this ev'ning light.

Chorus

Oh, what golden glory streaming!
  Purer light is coming fast;
Now in Christ we've found a freedom
  Which eternally shall last.

31 (271)

Back to the Blessed Old Bible

by
D. Otis Teasley (1907)

Back to the blessed old Bible, Back to the city of God,
  Back,to the oneness of heaven, Back where the faithful have trod.
Back from the land of confusion, Free from the bondage of creeds;
  Back to the light of the morning, Jesus our Captain leads.

Back to the blessed old Bible, Saints of Jehovah, rejoice;
  Jesus is calling his people, Back to the land of their choice.
Often our fathers had sought it, While they in Babel abode,
  Now we have found the fair city, Church of the living God.

Back to the blessed old Bible, Leaving confusion and strife;
  Fleeing from Babel to Zion, Back to the joy of our life.
Over the mountains we wandered, Looking in vain for the right,
  Now in the evening we've found it, Truth of the gospel light.

Back to the blessed old Bible, Back at the Master's call,
  Back to the Words of our Savior, Loving, obeying them all.
Never in sects to be scattered, Never again to do wrong:
  Unity, holiness, heaven, Ever shall be our song.

Refrain

Back to the blessed old Bible, Back to the Light of its word:
  Be on our banners forever, "Holiness unto the Lord."

A Child of God
by
B. E. Warren (1907)

Quoted from the *Hymnal of the Church of God*, Copyright
© 1971 by Warner Press, Inc.

Praise the Lord! my heart with his love is beaming,
    I am a child of God;
Heaven's golden light over me is streaming,
    I am a child of God.

Let the saints rejoice with my raptured spirit,
    I am a child of God;
I will testify that the world may hear it,
    I am a child of God.

Let a holy life tell the gospel story,
    I am a child of God;
How he fills the soul with his grace and glory,
    I am a child of God.

Saved from sin today, every band is riven,
    I am a child of God;
Thro' the tests of life I have peace from heaven,
    I am a child of God.

Refrain
I am a child of God, I am a child of God;
    I have washed my robes in the cleansing fountain,
I am a child of God.

The Reformation Glory

by
Charles W. Naylor (1922)

There's a mighty reformation sweeping o'er the land,
    God is gathering his people by his mighty hand;
For the cloudy day is ending and the evening sun is bright,
    With a shout of joy we hail the light.

When the voice from heaven sounded, warning all to flee
    From the darksome courts of Babel back to Zion free;
Glad my heart to hear the message, and I hastened to obey,
    And I'm standing in the truth today.

Zion's walls again are building as in days of yore,
    And the scattered hosts returning to their land once more
Are rejoicing in their freedom pledging evermore to stand
    In the reformation truths so grand.

Christians all should dwell together in the bonds of peace,
    All the clashing of opinions, all the strife should cease;
Let divisions be forsaken, all the holy join in one,
    And the will of God in all be done.

Refrain
O the reformation glory!
    Let it shine to every land:
We will tell the blessed story;
    In its truth we e'er shall stand.

O Church of God

by
Charles W. Naylor (1923)

Quoted from the *Hymnal of the Church of God*, Copyright
© 1971 by Warner Press, Inc.

The church of God one body is,
  One Spirit dwells within;
And all her members are redeemed,
  And triumph over sin.

Divinely built, divinely ruled,
  To God she doth submit;
His will her law, his truth her guide,
  Her path is glory-lit.

God sets her members each in place,
  According to his will—
Apostles, prophets, teachers, all,
  His purpose to fulfill.

In beauty stand, O church of God,
  With righteousness arrayed;
Put on thy strength and face thy foes
  With courage undismayed.

Refrain

O church of God! I love thy courts,
  Thou mother of the free;
Thou blessed home of all the saved,
  I dwell content in thee.

The Church's Jubilee
by
Charles W. Naylor (1923)

Quoted from the *Hymnal of the Church of God*, Copyright © 1971 by Warner Press, Inc.

The light of eventide now shines the darkness to dispel,
  The glories of fair Zion's state ten thousand voices tell;
For out of Babel God doth call his scattered saints in one,
  Together all one church compose, the body of his Son.

The Bible is our rule of faith and Christ alone is Lord,
  All we are equal in his sight when we obey his word;
No earthly master do we know, to man-rule will not bow,
  But to each other and to God eternal trueness vow.

The day of sects and creeds for us forevermore is past,
  Our brotherhood are all the saints upon the world so vast;
We reach our hands in fellowship to every blood-washed one,
  While love entwines about each heart in which God's will is done.

O blessed truth that broke our bonds! in it we now rejoice,
  While in the holy church of God we hear our Savior's voice;
And gladly to his blessed will submissive we shall be,
  And from the yokes of Babel's lords from henceforth we are free.

Refrain

O church of God, the day of jubilee
  Has dawned so bright and glorious for thee;
Rejoice, be glad! thy Shepherd has begun
  His long divided flock again to gather into one.

The Riggle-Kesler Debate
by
Herbert M. Riggle

Excerpted from *The Riggle-Kesler Debate*, by H. M. Riggle and B. E. Kesler (Anderson, Ind.: 1915).

Proposition

"The Church of the Brethren, of which I, B. E. Kesler, am a member, and which I represent, is identical with the New Testament Church in origin, name, doctrine, and practice."

B. E. Kesler affirms
H. M. Riggle denies

(Riggle)
I WILL NOW GIVE MY FINAL SUMMARY AND NEGATIVE ARGUMENTS:

First. I made the point that to be identical the Church of the Brethren must be THE SAME, DIFFERING IN NO ESSENTIAL POINT.

Second. I proved that there is no identity between the founders of these two churches.

The New Testament Church was founded by Christ (Matt. 16:18). Whereas the Church of the Brethren had its beginning in a small company of eight persons who met on the bank of the Eder in Schwarzenau, Germany, in the year 1708, at which time Elder Moore of the Brethren Church tells us "a new religious sect" had its beginning.

From these facts I presented the following logical conclusions:

A Time to Remember: TEACHINGS

(1) Christ built his own church, which he denominates "my church." Whereas the one built on the River Eder in Germany by eight fallible persons cannot be his church.

(2) The one is divine, the other human. The one was founded by the infallible God, the other by finite, fallible man. No identity.

(3) The New Testament Church was conceived in the divine mind, parallel with the gift of his Son. Its origin dates back to the plan of God from the foundation of the world. The law, its tabernacles and services, was the shadow of this church. Whereas, the Church of the Brethren was conceived in the human minds of eight fallible men, therefore, there can be no identity between the two bodies.

Third. There is no identity in the nature of the two bodies. The New Testament Church is a spiritual house (1 Pet. 2:5). The Church of the Brethren is a literal temporal structure, as men cannot manufacture spiritual things.

Fourth. The New Testament Church is the whole. It is the established church, the first of the Christian dispensation. It is no sect. Whereas the Church of the Brethren is admitted by Elder Moore and by Elder Kesler several times during this discussion to be a sect. Since a sect is a body dissenting from the established church, there cannot possibly be any identity between the two bodies.

Fifth. I proved that there is no identity between the New Testament Church and the Church of the Brethren as to date of organization. The New Testament Church began under the labors of John and continued during the ministry of Christ, and was fully organized in its completed perfected sense on Pentecost in A. D. 33. Whereas the Church of the Brethren dates from the years 1708, or 1675 years too late to be identical with the New Testament Church.

Sixth. There is no identity between the two bodies as to place of organization. The New Testament Church was organized at Jerusalem. This was by divine appointment. The prophet had foretold that the Word of the Lord would go forth from Jerusalem and Jesus instructed his disciples to tarry in Jerusalem until endued from on high, with the promise that they should be witnesses first in Jerusalem, then throughout all Judea, and finally unto the uttermost parts of the earth. Whereas the Church of the Brethren had its beginning near Schwarzenau, Germany, without any authority or prophetic truth pointing thereunto. Hence, without authority from the Word of God.

Seventh. I next proved that there is no identity between the two bodies in the manner of setting up the two institutions. Therefore they cannot possibly be the same.

To these logical and unanswerable facts which Elder Kesler could not refute, he simply replied that if Christ built one church why could he not build another? To this I replied that of the New Testament Church which Christ built it is declared would "never be destroyed," *and* "shall stand forever." And again, of the New Testament Church, Jesus said, "the gates of hell shall not prevail against it." Based upon this unanswerable fact, I presented this logical conclusion that since the New Testament Church is destined to stand forever, and is an exclusive church, it leaves no room for a rival body, and there is no need of any. There is absolutely no Scriptural proof that Christ would ever build more than the one divine church. Therefore, the sect known as the Church of the Brethren is without scriptural authority for its existence.

Eighth. I *clearly* proved that there is no identity between the New Testament Church and the Church of the Brethren in membership. Christ is the door of the former (John 10:9). Triune baptism is the door into the latter. Salvation makes us members of the New Testament Church (Acts 2:47). Salvation makes no one a member of the Church of the Brethren. The Lord adds the members and takes them into the New Testament Church (1 Cor. 12:13, 18). Whereas, by the literal rite of baptism, the preacher takes members into the Brethren sect. A Spiritual work inducts us into the Church whereas a literal rite inducts members into the Church of the Brethren. They cannot be the same.

Ninth. I clearly proved that the two bodies are not identical in their universality. The New Testament Church is declared to be the body of Christ, hence includes all Christians. Whereas the Church of the Brethren includes but a very small part of God's family. The two bodies, then, cannot be the same.

Tenth. I made the point that there is no need of this new body known as the Church of the Brethren. Because

(1) Christ built a perfect church that was to continue throughout all ages; hence no man can improve upon the divine system.

(2) In the days of the apostles they had perfect organization, visibility, and success, without this late rival body. There is no excuse for its existence.

Eleventh. I clearly proved that God had but one church under the old covenant, and that was the typical church, hence he has but one church under the new covenant, which is the antitypical church. Since Christ has but one true church, and this church existed seventeen centuries before the Church of the Brethren ever was heard of, this last institution which Elder Kesler represents cannot be Christ's church. To all this he replied that, since Christ built his church in Palestine, could he not build a distinct and separate body seventeen centuries later in Germany? Against this I gave the following fact and logical answer: The New Testament Church is the same in organization, visibility, membership, faith, doctrine and practice, in all nations, throughout all ages.

He next replied that the Church of the Brethren is now the same in all countries, therefore identical. I clearly proved that this establishes no identity, for it would prove as much for the Catholics and Mormons, who are the same in all countries.

Twelfth. I clearly proved that in every case where the plural term *churches* is used in the New Testament, it always applies to the local bodies or assemblies of God's people in different parts of the world who held membership in the one universal church. And that this plural term is never once used to represent distinct, separate bodies or churches.

Thirteenth. He tried to establish identity by saying that the

New Testament Church believed and taught faith, repentance, the new birth, baptism, holiness, sanctification, perfection, and so on, and that because the Church of the Brethren hold and teach these truths in some manner, the two bodies are identical. I showed the fallacy of his argument by proving that these are points of teaching which most all Christian people accept and, by his own logic, proves as much for the Mormons and the Catholics as it does for him.

Fourteenth. I clearly proved that the New Testament Church is the body of Christ, nothing more or nothing less (Col. 1:18, 24; Eph. 1:22-23). The Church of the Brethren cannot be the body of Christ, for Christ's body existed for seventeen centuries before the Church of the Brethren came into existence. They cannot be the same. The New Testament Church is one body. The New Testament only teaches and recognizes one body. Since the Church of the Brethren came seventeen hundred years later it has no recognition in the New Testament. It cannot be Christ's body.

Fifteenth. The New Testament Church is the house of God, the family of God, the bride, the Lamb's wife. The New Testament clearly teaches that Christ has but one house, one family, one bride. This leaves the Church of the Brethren without any identity, for it cannot be that one house, family and bride.

Sixteenth. I gave a prophetic history of the Church as portrayed in prophecy and Revelation and confirmed by the testimony of history. I thus traced it from its morning glory down through the twelve hundred and sixty years of popery, through the three hundred and fifty years of Protestant Sectism to its final restoration in the same unity, organization, faith, purity and power of primitive times; a blessed state now enjoyed by hundreds of thousands who are being gathered in the blessed evening light.

Thus, I established the identity of the church I have the honor to represent with that of the New Testament Church, and clearly proved that the organization named the Church of the Brethren has no place in prophetic record, unless indeed that it was foretold that sects would arise in which

God's people would be scattered.

Seventeenth. I clearly proved that the title, the Church of the Brethren, cannot be found in the New Testament. That the term *brethren*, as used there, is a universal term applying to all God's people in all ages, and is not limited to a certain distinct organization. I clearly showed that there are a number of other bodies as the United Brethren, Radical Brethren, Plymouth Brethren, Old Order Brethren, and Progressive Brethren, that have as much right to this title as the Elder's church.

I clearly proved that the New Testament Church was named by the mouth of the Lord. That God's people and city were to be called after his name. In the fulfillment Christ named the church after the Father, as the family of God and the bride of Christ. That this title by twelve clear texts of Scripture is declared to be the "*Church of God.*" Thus I have clearly proved that the Church of the Brethren is in no sense identical with the New Testament Church in origin or in name.

Four Basic
Pioneer Convictions
by
Adam W. Miller

Excerpted from *We Hold These Truths*, by Adam W. Miller (Anderson, Ind.: Mid-Century Evangelistic Advance, 1950).

BEHIND the general beliefs and practices of the movement are four basic convictions. They may be stated as follows:

1. Back to the Bible

There was a deliberate return to biblical revelation on the part of the early leaders. One of the familiar hymns states this conviction in these words:

Back to the blessed old Bible,
  Back at the Master's call,
Back to the words of our Savior,
  Loving, obeying them all.

Our early leaders recognized that the Christian world and its leaders had set the Bible aside as the revelation of God and were following a philosophy not in accord with that revelation. They were aware that in spite of nineteen hundred years of accumulated experience, the Christian world had fallen away from the original ideal. What that ideal was could best be determined by a deliberate return to Christ himself and his best interpreters, the apostles. The leaders of the movement sounded the cry, "Back to the Bible," because they were deeply convinced that New Testament Christianity could be realized in our day.

Such a seeking to return to apostolic days in quest of the ideal is a process that is scientific in the fullest sense. Just as natural science makes progress by perpetually returning to the reality of nature, so the church through its leaders and theologians advances by returning to reality. Christ is that great spiritual reality, and the best witness to him is to be found in the New Testament record.

Behind this drive to return to the ideals of the New Testament was the conviction of the movement's leaders that the Christian experience and life revealed in those writings could be reproduced in their day. This does not mean that they did not recognize that the background of early Christianity was Jewish and Greek. The message was expressed in ways that would be understood by the people of the first century. Yet within the New Testament form of expression are revealed an experience and a life so unique that they stand out above the culture and environment of that day. The gospel was so different that it could not be confused with anything else. Yet the Christian life and experience were such that they would be contemporaneous with every century, with every period, with every cultural situation.

2. Supernatural Religion

The second basic emphasis grew out of the first. Nominal Christianity was giving only lip service to the great doctrines of Christian experience, such as the new birth, entire sanctification, and the baptism of the Holy Spirit. These doctrines were in reality descriptions of great experiences of the soul. Before they were formulated and expressed as doctrines, they were experienced by men and women of that early period.

The pioneers of this movement knew only too well that other things were being substituted in practice for these great experiences. In some cases the truth for which these doctrines stood was rejected. Infant baptism, confirmation, adult baptism, joining the church, and a number of popular methods were used to bring people into association with the church.

The basic conviction of those early leaders was that Christian experience is supernatural. It results from the breaking through of God into human life. By the *new birth* or *regeneration* they meant that remarkable and extraordinary change that took place in a man's moral nature, breaking the power of sin and changing the whole direction of his life. This was something done by God through the operation of the Holy Spirit upon a man's inward nature. Freedom from sin was then possible, and holiness of life resulted.

Entire sanctification, they discovered, was an instantaneous work of grace, which came to the Christian as an experience subsequent to the experience of the new birth. The incoming or baptism of the Holy Spirit was the positive aspect of this experience. The term "sanctification" expressed the idea of cleansing or purification. It stood for or expressed another step in the process of making a man holy.

The incoming of the Holy Spirit meant that God took up his abode in the human life, and that life now became an instrument of the dynamic power of the Spirit.

The very descriptions of these experiences immediately reveal their supernatural quality. Man did not and could not do these things for himself. Someone, a power outside a man, namely God himself, came to do this in man and for man, and finally came to dwell in man's soul as the Holy Spirit.

The implications of these experiences are tremendous. Holiness is possible only through such supernatural experiences, coming to man as the gifts of God. The continuation of the work of God in the world results from the operation of the Spirit of God in his people—the church. Charismatic bestowals or endowments come through this same Spirit. Charismatic leadership also is possible only through the Spirit.

3. The Church as the Body of Christ

Perhaps one of the most basic convictions which found emphasis in the preaching and teaching of those early leaders was the concept of the church as the body of Christ which they discovered within the pages of the New Testament.

They found that in the New Testament the church was the totality of those who knew Christ and in whom Christ dwelt. There they found the church set forth as consisting of all who have accepted the salvation which is in Christ. They saw that the bond of union among the members is the Holy Spirit who fills the body. The church is *one* because it is the body of Christ, and because every member is necessary to all the rest. It is united, not by offices or officials, not by documentary constitution or creed, not by a priestly or episcopal order but by the fellowship of the Spirit.

The New Testament church was the community of the saints. The test of membership was the divine life each one had in Christ Jesus. There was no other condition of membership.

A Time to Remember: TEACHINGS

In returning to the New Testament for the ideal of the church, the movement's early leaders were aware that there had been a falling away from the ideal through the centuries. They were also aware of some of the steps by which men left the simplicity of the New Testament teaching and set up a pattern of a church quite different from that revealed in the Word of God.

The early leaders of the Church of God movement were students of the process by which the idea of the church was changed. They were familiar with the process, not only as it developed into the Roman church, but also as it was reflected in the varying concepts of Protestant churches.

It was against such a background that the leaders of the movement deliberately sought to return to the simple ideal of the New Testament and to work for its realization.

4. The Vision of Christian Unity

Their search for the New Testament ideals led those early leaders to see that the ultimate goal of the gospel is a unified church. I think what they saw as a result of their study of the New Testament might well be expressed in the following statement which I have adapted for my present use:

"The vision which rises before us is that of a church, genuinely universal, loyal to all truth, and gathering in its fellowship all who are truly Christians, within whose visible unity all the treasures of faith shall be possessed in common by the whole body of Christ."

They had a sure foundation for their ideal of unity in the prayer of Christ: "That they all may be one; as thou, Father, art in me, and I in thee, that they also may be one in us: that the world may believe that thou hast sent me. . . . I in them, and thou in me, that they may be made perfect in one; and that the world may know that thou hast sent me, and hast loved them, as thou hast loved me" (John 17:21-23).

46 (286)

What the Pioneers Preached
by
John W. V. Smith

Excerpted from *Truth Marches On*, by John W. V. Smith (Anderson, Ind.: Gospel Trumpet Company, Copyright © 1956).

"The God of Peace Sanctify You Wholly" (1 Thess. 5:23)

One of the first principles set forth by these nineteenth-century reformers was that every genuine Christian ought to live a life that was holy. The holy life was defined as one free from outward sin and also free from any inward intention to do wrong. That they expected all within their fellowship to live up to this standard is evidenced by the fact that from the beginning they spoke of themselves as "the saints." This was not a title to be attached to a select few of the holy people of the past but a descriptive term applying to the living company of those who, here and now, were fully controlled by the Holy Spirit.

Such a state could not be achieved by purely natural means, however. Even as it was impossible for man to be redeemed except as he accepted the supernatural work of God through Jesus Christ, so also it was not possible for a person to live a holy life in his own strength. He must have supernatural assistance, and this was available when one would take a second step in his spiritual experience and accept the sanctifying work of the Holy Spirit.

The importance of the doctrine of sanctification in the minds of the pioneers can hardly be overexaggerated. If a single truth were to be designated as the basic root from which the reformation sprang, this would probably be considered most basic. Many sermons, articles, and tracts expounded this truth at great length. D.S. Warner began his editorial career in 1878 when he was put in charge of the holiness department of the *Herald of Gospel Freedom*. His first book, published in 1880 before there was a *Gospel Trumpet*, was entitled, *Bible Proofs of a Second Work of Grace*. It was through contacts made in the preaching of this doctrine that many of the early leaders in the Church of God reformation were brought together.

In the early writing and preaching on sanctification two points stand out clearly. The first is that sanctification is a divine work, wrought by the Holy Spirit, and that it alters a man's very nature. It is not something which man can do for himself, so it cannot be identified with the blessing one receives in making a deeper consecration or a more complete submission to the divine will. The second point is that sanctification is a complete work. Entire sanctification meant an elevation of life to the plane that even one's motives and desires were made perfect and were brought into harmony with the will of God. This did not preclude growth in knowledge and understanding nor improvement in conduct, for these would continue as long as one lived, but it did demand a life that was free from any carnal intention.

"Be Not Conformed to This World" (Rom. 12:2)

The doctrine of holiness was not an abstract theological concept to these early leaders; it was a practical standard for everyday living. Positively, holiness was defined as a life under the complete direction of the Holy Spirit. Negatively it was defined as nonconformity to the world. This required that "worldliness" be defined. The pioneers were very practical-minded, so they were not content with a general definition. They sought to be specific, so they named particular practices and procedures which were considered worldly and were to be avoided by the saints. In general, the items included were of the same nature as the ascetic disciplines imposed by other Christian groups greatly concerned about personal piety. The chief areas in which definitions seemed necessary were those of food, dress, amusements, and relationships to society.

It is neither possible nor necessary at this point to enumerate all the items which were included in these definitions. Partaking of certain foods and beverages was declared to be wrong because they were considered harmful to the body. It was on this basis that tea and coffee were under condemnation for a number of years. Because tight-fitting corsets were considered injurious to health they were also condemned. The majority of the regulations involving dress were attempts to avoid any indications of vanity or pride. During the early 1900s women were asked to forego lace and ruffles, and the men were expected to leave off their neckties. The wearing of gold and other ornaments was considered worldly adornment. Most forms of professional entertainment were regarded as sinful, and anything more than a mild interest in public affairs was considered an overconcern with the things of this world.

A backward look at some of these matters may provoke a few smiles and may even make one wonder why there was so much concern over seemingly small matters. To these people, however, such standards were far from being small matters. They were seeking a tangible means of indicating their separation from the world. These were the marks of distinction that would help them convey their witness. They were earnest and sincere men and women who wanted more than anything else to be faithful to their high calling as children of God. The standards and discipline which they imposed upon themselves were born out of a deep conviction that these were necessary in order to be true to God's demands.

"Come Out . . . and Be Ye Separate" (2 Cor. 6:17)

The early leaders of the Church of God reformation were sometimes called "come-outers" because they advocated the withdrawal of all true Christians from the various sects and denominations in which they were scattered and divided. These pioneers believed it was possible to reconstitute the church of the New Testament by inviting all who had been spiritually reborn to enter into a fellowship which was not restricted by any of the organizational or creedal limitations which had been established by the existing churches. One of the early congregations drew up a resolution which declared, "We adhere to no body or organization but the church of God, bought by the blood of Christ, organized by the Holy Spirit, and governed by the Bible."

In taking such a stand these people were careful to make it clear that they were not starting another sect. Their intention was quite to the contrary. They, indeed, were providing an escape from sectism. Instead of organizing another "church among the churches" they were issuing a call to all true Christians to shake off the secondary allegiances which were keeping them apart and to join in this movement to restore the church to its intended purity and unity.

Scriptural support for "come-outism" the early leaders found in many Old Testament warnings that Israel should avoid contamination by their idol-worshiping neighbors. In the New Testament Paul quotes one of these passages (Isa. 52:11) and uses it to admonish the Corinthians to keep themselves free from the sinful paganism with which they were surrounded. To the pioneers of the Church of God reformation these Scripture passages were perfectly applicable. Sectism was sin. It was to be forsaken just like anything else sinful. One could not be genuinely Christian and participate in this sinful division of the body of Christ. The only logical course was to "come out" from these ungodly sectarian organizations into the true church of God.

"The Lord Added to the Church" (Acts 2:47)

Pioneer leaders of the Church of God movement were convinced that the various systems of church joining allowed many unworthy people to become affiliated with what was supposed to be a divine institution. They searched the Scriptures for clear guidance as to the proper method for admitting people into the church. They found no procedure outlined and no method recommended, but they did find that the church is a divine institution. The more they studied, the more apparent it became that no man has the right to set the boundaries of the church. Neither is it the right of any man or any group to declare who is in or who is out of the church. God alone can do that. Church membership procedures, then, are nothing more than humanly devised ceremonies and have little or no relationship to real membership in the church.

In order to avoid the error of presuming to do God's judging for him these reformers declared that one becomes a member of the church when he experiences the new birth. No rite or ceremony is necessary to admit one into the divine fellowship. As soon as one's sins are forgiven, he at that moment enters the brotherhood of the redeemed. The genuineness of that conversion experience is a matter for God alone to decide. The visible fellowship is made up of all those who testify that this divine work has been accomplished in their own souls.

"Now Hath God Set the Members . . . in the Body" (1 Cor. 12:18)

One of the most apparent aspects of the early preaching in the Church of God movement was the horror which the leaders had for all types of humanly devised organization in the church. There were two reasons why they felt this way. The first was a continuation of their belief that the church was a divine institution and was not subject to human structuring. The second was a burning conviction that the Holy Spirit had been designated as the full governing agency of the church and any attempt at "man rule" was sheer interference with the divine plan.

Looking back on this period from the vantage point of the present we might wonder why these people were so afraid of organization. As one examines the sermons and writings of the leaders, however, he discovers that they had a very clear understanding of the real nature of the church's difficulties. They could see that many of the barriers existing between Christians were due to the fact that each group followed after its own peculiar notions and developed loyalty to its own system rather than to Christ alone. They could also see that practically none of the organizational systems left much room for the operation of the Holy Spirit.

Their real fear, then, was not of organization as such but of humanly devised organization without the control of the Holy Spirit. To keep from falling into the error of "man rule" they resolved to develop no system of their own to which people might attach their allegiance and to keep all organization at a minimum. This, they felt, would give the Holy Spirit opportunity to work more directly and accomplish his will more completely, since there was no highly developed system to get in the way.

"That They All May Be One" (John 17:21)

It might at first seem that all these points of special emphasis were unrelated to each other and even incidental to the central truth of the Christian gospel which is obviously that God sent his Son into the world to save sinners. Upon closer examination, however, it is discovered that all of these point directly to this central truth, in that all of them are concerned with the characteristics of the company of the redeemed—the church. To these five truths the pioneers added another great affirmation which brought their whole message into sharper focus. This crowning emphasis was the firm conviction that God intended for all his people to be united in one fellowship.

This meant that the early leaders were not content to point to the error and sin of division. They did not stop with an invitation to "come out" of the sects. They went a step further and sought to demonstrate that a real visible unity of the church was an achievable ideal. The accomplishment of this goal, they said, could never be reached by applying external pressures, by developing a super organization, or by compromising differences. It was possible only as people were brought together by sharing in the common experience of redemption through Jesus Christ, were willing to open themselves to all truth, and measured their lives according to their full understanding of the will of God. A unity achieved on this basis would be true and genuine, for it would grow out of a real unity of spirit rather than being some kind of union imposed upon people who were not really together at heart.

The Church of God reformation movement was more than a series of emphases, however. It was a crusade to open the door of all truth. Some of the specific content of this truth was lifted up and proclaimed, but the limits of truth were never defined. That was left open, for God was still at work among his people, and who could say when the boundaries of his revelation had been reached?

Carson City Resolutions

Excerpted from *Birth of a Reformation*, by Andrew L. Byers (Anderson, Ind.: Gospel Trumpet Company, Copyright © 1921). Reprinted by Faith Publishing House, Guthrie, Okla.

TWO CONGREGATIONS of saints—at Beaver Dam, (Ind.), and Carson City, (Mich.),—were the earliest in the United States (so far as the author knows) who had stepped completely out of Babylon and had taken for their basis that of the New Testament church alone. An annual camp meeting was established at each place.

The Michigan saints in order to express in definite form their position and intentions drew up the following resolutions:

Whereas we recognize ourselves in the perilous times of the last days, the time in which Michael is standing up for the deliverance of God's true saints (Dan. 12:1), the troublesome times in which the true house of God is being built again, therefore.

Resolved, That we will endeavor by all the grace of God to live holy, righteous, and godly in Christ Jesus, "looking for, and hastening unto the coming of the Lord Jesus Christ," who we believe is nigh, even at the door.

Resolved, That we adhere to no body or organization but the church of God, bought by the blood of Christ, organized by the Holy Spirit, and governed by the Bible. And if the Lord will, we will hold an annual assembly of all saints who in the providence of God shall be permitted to come together for the worship of God, the instruction and edification of one another, and the transaction of such business as the Holy Spirit may lead us to see and direct in its performance.

Resolved, That we ignore and abandon the practise of preacher's license as without precept or example in the Word of God, and that we wish to be "known by our fruits" instead of by papers.

Resolved, That we do not recognize or fellowship any who come unto us assuming the character of a minister whose life is not godly in Christ Jesus and whose doctrine is not the Word of God.

Resolved also, That we recognize and fellowship, as members with us in the one body of Christ, all truly regenerated and sincere saints who worship God in all the light they possess, and that we urge all the dear children of God to forsake the snares and yokes of human parties and stand alone in the "one fold" of Christ upon the Bible, and in the unity of the Spirit.

Theological Self-Identifications

The following are theological self-identifications of the *Gospel Trumpet (Vital Christianity)*, drawn from sample issues of four different historical periods.

January 3, 1895: Gospel Trumpet

> DEFINITE, RADICAL, and ANTI-SECTARIAN, sent forth in the name of the Lord Jesus Christ, for the publication of full Salvation, and Divine Healing

of the Body, the Unity of all true Christians in "the faith once delivered to the saints."

January 2, 1930: Gospel Trumpet

A Definite, Heart-Searching, Non-Sectarian Religious Weekly Published in the Interests of the Church of God, For the salvation of sinners, entire sanctification of believers, divine healing of the body, and the unity of all true Christians in "the faith once delivered to the saints."

January 7, 1950: Gospel Trumpet

A Weekly Journal of Vital Christianity published in the interests of the Church of God, for the salvation of sinners, entire sanctification of believers, divine healing of the body, and the unity of all true Christians in "the faith once delivered to the saints."

January 5, 1975: Vital Christianity

(Does not state a theological self-identification in the format of the above statements, but indicative of the magazine's current stance is this statement by Editor Arlo F. Newell, which appeared in the context of his editorial for the October 30, 1977 issue:)

Warner Press has a responsibility to speak through the printed page to the vital issues of the day. Because of our theology, we should be able to deal not in a biased manner, but very openly from the biblical perspective, presenting God's Word for the needs of all persons. As a publishing house, we should be in touch with the present concerns of our society, leading the way in producing articles and materials that deal with these concerns rather than following after what others have already produced.

Our Basic Convictions

Excerpted from *So This Is the Church of God*, published in 1969 by the Executive Council of the Church of God.

CHURCH OF GOD people have some dreams. They are in many ways a visionary people. These dreams affect what they believe and how they serve. To consider the nature of these dreams we would ask: What do Church of God people believe? How are they like or unlike people of other religious groups?

These dreams have, across the years, centered around several central hopes. There is the dream that men might be won to Christ and find their salvation in him. There is the dream that Christians might serve their Lord in the spirit of unity. And there is the dream that men might find power and purity through the Holy Spirit to live extraordinary lives under Christ's lordship. These are dreams that find their base in the teachings of the Bible.

Since Church of God people seek to base their lives and teachings so strongly in Scripture, consider the Bible and the part it plays in the Church of God. Here the movement shares in the common Protestant heritage of putting great emphasis on this book and its authority for the individual believer. For him it outranks church tradition, present-day common customs of society, and creedal statements as a source of guidance and insight into the nature and will of God. It is a book to be studied, meditated upon, used much, and heeded.

Even so, the Bible is not regarded as a book to be worshiped for itself alone. It takes on its value in bringing to us the inspired message from God. While the most unlettered and ignorant of persons can read this book and gain inspiration and insight from it, the Bible is also worthy of the most exacting scholarly pursuit and is deserving of the most accurate kind of interpretation. Principles of interpretation like the following are seen to apply. One would not base a major doctrine on an isolated verse but would study the Bible in larger passages, in light of the historical setting and the original audience to which the particular book involved was addressed. The teachings indicated in a given passage would be checked against the main trend of teaching in the Bible. While the whole Bible is honored, the New Testament takes on direct significance with the Old understood as prologue. The Church of God calls itself a "New Testament" church, not because it disavows the Old Testament but because it sees the cardinal teachings of the Bible (as about the church) coming to their fulfillment in the New. People in the Church of God seek to base their understanding of doctrine on the most clear and central teachings of the Bible. Rather than a traditional or orthodox or liberal theology constructed out of trends in philosophy or moods of the times Church of God people seek a biblical theology.

Such a theology leads Church of God people to affirm their belief in God. Generally, however, they do not arrive at a concept of him out of philosophical reasoning or doctrinal study as much as from the conviction that they have personal relationships with this God through prayer and meditation and through sensing him at work—redeeming his people and sustaining his world.

They seek to keep as full a vision of God as is possible in our limited human situation without being trapped into the too-narrow views that may hedge people in. Here is not only a personal God intimately concerned with us and the details of our lives but also the great God who rules the universe. Here is not a God who becomes merely a part of his creation but is always over and above it. Here is a just God, a forgiving God, a loving God, a healing God, a renewing, creating God. Here is a God who has created us in his own likeness to share freely in fellowship with him. Here is not a God who is an errand boy, a quaint old grandfather type, a legalist, or a favorites-player. Here is the great God who loves us.

By understanding God as one who has personal interest in them, Church of God people look to God for healing power. The current widespread interest in spiritual healing is no new thing in this movement where divine healing has been emphasized across the years. The God who healed people in Bible times is the same today. Of course, God works through the healing hands of a physician or a nurse and through the new knowledge of science in this field, but he is still seen as a God who works daily miracles beyond the miracles of science. He is still the God who cares about the personal well-being of his children.

If the beliefs of Church of God people come to a central focus anywhere it is in Jesus Christ himself. They see him as a real and historical figure in the history of civilization but at the same time the divine son of God. He came to earth to redeem mankind, to bring us salvation. Here the movement's strong emphasis on evangelism takes root. Christ has come for our salvation, and the church is seen as an instrument of salvation. Man, caught in a web of sin and rebellion, is called to respond to Christ, to come to him in repentance and sorrow for his past sins, and to accept the redemption Christ offers. In an act of commitment, man is invited to make of himself a follower of Christ and to live in Christ's style of life.

Here Church of God people find themselves among the more evangelical Protestants. While there are vast social implications in the redemption God brings to the world through Christ, the general view of people in the Church of God—as among most other of the more evangelical and conservative groups—is that at its heart redemption is an intensely personal thing. Personal salvation must come. With this, through highly committed individual Christians whose consciences have been made sensitive, the big social issues can be met.

The Church of God movement, born in the midst of a revival of concern with holy living in the last century, has always given a major place to the Holy Spirit and his work. This is in some contrast to the place the Spirit has traditionally occupied in Christian history. Major movements and creeds have often had a hard time to make place for the Spirit even while they have held to a full-orbed view of the Trinity—Father, Son, and Holy Spirit. Stress on the work of the Spirit has often been left in the Christian tradition to relatively small groups who have sought consciously to keep strong their first-century ties and New Testament theology.

At any rate the Church of God has tried to be sensitive to the Holy Spirit at work—in the church, in society, among individuals—to make men whole, to sanctify them, to cleanse them, to empower them, to guide them. In short, the Spirit brings to Christians a "plus quality" for their living. Here men are equipped, not through any special merit or talent of their own, for living a life beyond their own powers and abilities. It is the dream of Church of God people that they can live such a life and point the way for others, not as holier-than-thou persons who draw their peculiar robes of righteousness about them but as people with good news to share and a vision of what it is all about. Such a dream does not remove them from society with its hungers, pressures, and weaknesses, but it does open to them a view of what can be done beyond human power with the empowering of the Spirit.

One common concern of Christian people around the world is for the unity of all Christians within the body of Christ. Such a concern seems almost impossible to realize when considering all the things that operate against it. There are the natural divisions of people, by the ways they think, by their social and cultural levels, by surface physical variations, by their sexes, by educational differences, by national loyalties and customs. The Church of God movement has taken this concern about unity seriously. Some of its specific practices and actions reflect this:

The name "Church of God" came into common usage in the movement as a designation that would not be the sort to distinguish it from any other group. Here was simply a biblical name for the church, one showing God's ownership, one which all Christians could rally around and be true to the New Testament.

The practice of not having formal church membership was another reflection of this concern for unity. It was felt from the beginning of the movement that to require people to go through a ceremony of joining the Church of God reformation movement apart from simply becoming a Christian was to raise additional sectarian barriers among Christians. Therefore, all persons who become genuinely Christian are regarded as full members of the church and as one with all other genuine Christians.

The practice of not having any creed but the central teachings of the Bible reflects another effort at not raising barriers between Christians. All Christians earnestly seeking to find all the truth they can in the Bible and to live by that draw nearer to Christ. As they do that, it is often said in the Movement, they find themselves drawing much nearer to each other.

Much of the movement's resistance to structuring itself ecclesiastically comes from this desire to be at one with all Christians. It was felt across the years that to develop complex churchly machinery would be to set up a structure that inevitably would come into competition with other groups and would be itself a body to fight for its own existence apart from the main body of Christ. There is, to be sure, a delicate line the movement struggles to follow here. Organization to get Christian work done is vital and is good stewardship. At the same time perfectly good organizations can become self-serving machinery if they do not remain dedicated under God to accomplishing his purposes.

It is at this point that much of the movement's question as to whether it can be allied with various Christian organizations arises. The Church of God does not belong to the National Council of Churches, the World Council of

Churches, or to the National Association of Evangelicals. There are those who feel that it does not have the legal machinery by which to join such organizations if it would. Yet for most of this century the movement has in one way or another been affiliated with cooperative religious enterprises. Local congregations and ministers often belong to city associations. Sometimes they belong to the parallel state organizations. Various general agencies of the church belonged to most of the cooperative national agencies in the fields of missions, stewardship, and Christian education which went together to form the National Council of Churches. Working relations with a number of National Council divisions have been maintained without formal membership in the Council itself. Such contacts have been viewed as essential in getting major tasks accomplished that could not have been carried on by small religious groups separately. These ties have been viewed as opportunity for people of the Church of God to offer their own witness, to learn new methods of work, and to demonstrate an open, ongoing spirit of unity.

Church of God people have a vision of the church, founded by Christ, with all his people added to it by Christ alone, a fellowship of the redeemed. The church is seen as intended to be one, as indeed it is one in spirit. Division is regarded as evil. The church becomes visible in the life and work of its people, this cropping out not only in the life of a local congregation but also in cooperative work on national, state, world, and local levels. The church shows up, too, not only in the organized life and worship of the congregation but also through the ministry of all its people day by day out in the world.

Experience with and obedience to Christ become important to those who would follow him. Lip service to Christian ideals is not enough. Affiliating oneself with other Christians is not enough. There are some symbolic acts of obedience and experience with Christ that are commonly practiced in the Church of God. When one becomes a Christian he makes a public testimony to this new relationship with Christ through baptism. This is the baptism of believers by immersion in water after they have reached an age of accountability. A high experience of worship for the Christian is the Lord's Supper, where the bread symbolizes Christ's body broken for us and the wine (our practice is to use unfermented grape juice) symbolizes his blood shed for us. The communion table is open to all persons who would honestly draw near to Christ. A third commonly practiced custom of this sort, symbolizing obedience and practical humble service to one's brother and the servant role of the church, is foot washing, traditionally observed on Maundy Thursday evening during Holy Week by separate groups of men and women. This follows long-held custom dating back through the history of the church to the Upper Room itself.

But, symbolic acts of obedience are, of course, not enough, important as they may be to the life and worship of the church. Church of God people are called to go forth on mission in behalf of the church, to bear witness to the will of God, and to exercise lives of stewardship. Stewardship involves the person in regarding his possessions not as really his own but as something placed in his keeping by God. There is the stewardship of his own body, as he seeks to keep it in as good health as he can. There is the stewardship of his talents, as he is called to develop these and use them for the good of his fellowman and in the service of Christ. There is the stewardship of material possessions and the money he controls. Here biblical example would suggest that a minimum of a tithe or 10 percent—and in most situations considerably more than that—would be given to the church out of a personal income. There is stewardship of time, and again the biblical example calls for Christians to give their time to unselfish causes rather than selfish interests.

Christians feel, even if they are not giving themselves to full-time church-related vocations, that they are sent out into the world on mission in behalf of Christ and his principles. Out there in the world they will be living as good a Christian example as they can. They will be talking about their faith, not in a pious or obnoxious way but in an enthusiastic winning style that is contagious. They will be taking their stands with Christian views on the pressing issues of the day. They will be ministering to people in spiritual and physical and social need. They will be fighting evil in any form that it may take in their communities. Many will be volunteering large blocks of their time to serve their needy brethren around the world. Church of God people are increasingly putting their muscles, sweat, and toil, where they say their hearts are.

Accompanying outward acts of obedience is the kind of high moral and ethical life that reflects what Christ has done for a person. Given full reign in a person's life, Christ brings to that life an inner radiance, an underlying peace, and a high sensitivity to what is right and what is wrong. Usually a religious group develops a culture pattern of practices in personal daily living, and the Church of God movement demonstrates this. Behavior patterns here generally agree with those demonstrated by other conservative religious groups. Use of alcoholic beverages and tobacco are regarded as harmful both to the individual's body and to the welfare of society. Sensitivities in this area spread also to a concern about the harmfulness of overeating or other kinds of personal overindulgence. The movement speaks out against gambling, against pornographic literature, and against the common immoralities of the society. It believes that recreational and leisure-time activities should be chosen with the greatest of care for what they may do to the human personality and to relationships with other Christians and with God.

Beyond such matters as these that seem to fit into a commonly accepted code of personal behavior, a number of questions are left to the sensitive conscience. Such is the approach to participation in war and the military life. Most young Church of God men participate in the military without question (and a number of ministers serve in its chaplaincy). Another group are supported in their position of conscientious objection to war and nonparticipation in the military. To the educated Christian conscience and taste are left matters of dress and many similar matters.

A growing emphasis is given to living positively in the spirit of God rather than under the direction of negative legalisms. Sins of the spirit are seen as more basic detriments to the Christian life than many items of failing to conform outwardly to a rigid set of dress or behavior standards. The big thing is to move into the life of abundance as disciples of Jesus Christ.

Yes, Church of God people have dreams, dreams that lead them to exalted beliefs and high standards for daily living. Sometimes they do not live up to their dreams, but vision is still out there beckoning them on to higher ground.

Let There Be Fellowship

Excerpted from the Committee on Christian Unity's report to the General Assembly, June 1967.

IN CONVERSATIONS with the Churches of God in North America we have stated with candor our position with regard to organic union. Each meeting with these brethren has given us fresh opportunity to exalt scriptural unity as a "more excellent way" than mere merger or organization. At the same time, the conversations have demanded of us such expressions of good faith as would show the Churches of God that our emphasis on unity is more than talk.

Our unwillingness to sacrifice basic convictions has tested the sincerity of their committee (and perhaps at times even frustrated them). At the same time they have demonstrated their openness, at the sacrifice of neither their integrity nor our fellowship. They have repeatedly found agreement with our position, actually being surprised that so little separates us.

Your committee has confessed every doctrinal position delivered to this reformation. Even when conflict might be anticipated we have approached the Churches of God with clear statements of our belief (acknowledging that no one of us speaks for all of us at any given point). Since we have never envisioned an eclectic theology bringing the two movements together, we felt compelled to say "this we believe . . . this we proclaim." There have been free discussions about the work of the Holy Spirit, the second coming, the ordinances, and other teachings common to and dissimilar to the two communions.

Your committee has been concerned to stay in the "mainstream" of this movement's understanding of the nature of the church. We felt this strategic to our work, whether responding to other groups or addressing our own pastors and congregations. Writings of our earlier theologians have been researched and contemporary scholars have been asked to present papers. We have felt at liberty to speak within the framework of what has been commonly held true among us.

Plainly the church is comprised of twice-born, not one less and not one more. This is hardly a revolutionary concept to the Churches of God in North America, who like to feel they contributed to D. S. Warner's understanding at this point. It has, however, been for us to apply the implications of the above simple truth: If membership in God's church is by conversion further "joining" obscures the primacy of the church universal.

D. S. Warner wrote, "The church, then, is organized by the Lord . . . Men may organize a human concept, but never the divine body of Christ which is the church . . . " (*The Church of God or What Is the Church and What Is Not,* page 11). Your committee is concerned with preserving the essentiality of this position.

Your committee has jealously guarded the Lordship of Christ as "head of the church." However, we have not ignored the possibilities inherent in appropriate organization. Christ may indeed have more preeminence where things are done "decently and in order" than where there is disruptive, selfish independence, or where there is a will to work but no coordination.

In our conversations, we have projected the church as a divine institution, divinely governed but conspicuously dependent upon man for "oversight" in its congregational functions. Man may participate in the mission of the church and is indeed expected to do so, often mapping strategy and exercising authority according to the measure of his revelation and ability.

According to R. R. Byrum, "The Spirit of God accomplishes his will in ruling his church through human instrumentality. The Spirit not only uses the elders especially, in ruling the church, but also operates through the various members of the congregation for the same purpose" (*Christian Theology,* page 530).

It has not been difficult for the Committee to account for our present structure. We could accept any structure clearly as organization of the *work* of the church and not of the *church* itself. Notwithstanding, in that administration of the church concerning the "setting of the members in the body" we contend for the authority of God.

In the final analysis it has seemed to our committee that Holy Spirit leadership is best served by attention to the "grass roots" of the church. If God is in this accord between the Churches of God in North America and us, it will be apparent to our people on the local level. The committee has no confidence in a decreed unity or a contrived unity. We have long been aware of the failure of hierarchies to properly interpret the "good and acceptable and perfect will of God."

Let the people *pray* and let the *people* speak. Let there be fellowship between the local pastors and the local congregations of the two movements. The church is not divinely governed when in a state of paralysis. Her cues come from God only when she moves out into encounter with danger and opportunity. It is to explorers only that he says, "This is the way."

All Believers Included

Quoted from the 1976-1977 catalogue of Alberta Bible Institute, Camrose, Alberta.

THE CHURCH OF GOD (Anderson, Indiana) is a movement in the direction of Christian unity, emphasizing New Testament standards of faith and practice without adhering to a formal written creed or statement of faith. The movement declares itself open to new truth and encourages a spirit of inquiry in that direction under the guidance and illumination of the Holy Spirit.

Therefore the following is written to briefly indicate the general position of the movement and is not intended to be binding or authoritative. It is hoped that this will inform those who are interested in the basic doctrinal position of the college.

We believe:
1.   the Scriptures, both Old and New Testaments, to be the inspired Word of God, the revelation of his will for the salvation of men, and the divine authority for all Christian faith and life;
2.   in one God, Creator of all things, infinitely perfect and eternally co-existing in three Persons, Father, Son and Holy Spirit;
3.   that Jesus Christ is the Son of God, truly divine and truly human, conceived of the Holy Spirit and born of the virgin Mary; that he died on the cross, a sacrifice for our sins; that he was resurrected bodily from the dead, ascended into heaven, where at the right hand of the Majesty on high, he is now our High Priest and Advocate;
4.   that the ministry of the Holy Spirit is to glorify the Lord Jesus Christ at all times. He is working in the conviction and salvation of sinners and the sanctification of believers

to indwell, instruct, and empower for godly living and Christian service;

5. that man was created in the image of God but through disobedience fell out of fellowship with God, and that only by salvation through the atonement of Jesus Christ can he be reconciled to God by faith;

6. that the true Church of God is composed of all redeemed persons, who through faith in Jesus Christ are united together in the body of Christ of which he is head. We believe in the royal priesthood of believers, in the exercise of divine healing and spiritual gifts in the church;

7. that the kingdom of God is a spiritual kingdom being established in the hearts and lives of believers as they acknowledge the lordship of Jesus Christ, and that this kingdom shall increase through the proclamation of the good news of salvation until the end of the age culminating in the Second Coming of Christ, the resurrection of the dead and the final Judgment.

What We Believe

by
A. T. Rowe

Excerpted from the *Gospel Trumpet,* January 6, 1898.

AS THE TRUMPET is now reaching many new homes, I have felt impressed to write a few lines on what we believe, because so many false religions and false ideas as to what we believe are extant in the land.

1. We believe in justification by faith, which gives us peace with God and frees us from all committed or actual sins (Rom. 5:1).
2. We believe in sanctification by faith, as a second definite instantaneous work of grace, which frees us from the inherited, or adamic, sin (1 John 1:7; Titus 3:5; John 15:2).
3. We believe we must live a life free from sin in this present world (1 John 3:9, 5:18; Titus 2:11-12). God cleanses us from all desire or love for sin, but we are not infallible; neither is it impossible for us to sin, nor make a mistake, nor err in judgment.
4. We believe we will be subject to temptation as long as we remain in this world, but God will give us grace to resist temptation (1 Cor. 10:12-13).
5. We do not believe, as is commonly spoken, that we *must* sin in thought, word, and deed; as there are no other ways to sin, and the mission of Jesus to this world was to save us from sin (Matt. 1:21; Ps. 103:3; Titus 2:11-14).
6. We believe in being called individually by the name *saint,* the meaning of which is a saved person; and as a body, the name *church of God* (Acts 20:28; 1 Tim. 3:15; 1 Cor. 1:2).
7. We believe this name applies to both the visible and the invisible part of the church (Eph. 3:14-15).
8. We are not Latter-day Saints, do not accept the Book of Mormon, nor Joseph Smith as a prophet of God. We do not believe in plural marriage, free-lovism, promiscuous feet-washing, or kissing (that is, with the opposite sex while observing these ordinances), and do not practice any such things.
9. We have no discipline or government outside of the Bible; yet we believe in church government as set forth in Isa. 9:6; 1 Cor. 12:18; Eph. 4:11-14.
10. We believe in equality eldership, and that God calls, qualifies, ordains, and sends his ministers; and he himself equips them with authority to preach, baptize,

anoint the sick, administer the ordinances, or any other duty enjoined upon them.

11. We have no conference except that from above, receive no stated salary, take no basket collections; and our circuit extends to the whole world (Mark 16:15).

12. We believe there is only one church, and that God is calling his people out of all divisions into the one body, which is Jesus Christ (2 Cor. 6:14-18; Rev. 18:4).

13. We believe that there are saved people in sectism, and that many have died while there and were saved; but that God has designed that his people should worship together, believe the same thing, and worship under one name (1 Cor. 1:10; Phil. 1:27; Matt. 18:20).

14. We keep no class-book, or record of members, but believe it is sufficient to have our names recorded in heaven (Luke 10:20; Heb. 12:22-23; Rev. 20:15).

15. We accept as the ordinances of the church:

    1st. Baptism by immersion, or burial (Col. 2:12; John 3:23; Acts 8:38). We fail to find one scripture favoring either pouring or sprinkling.

    2nd. Feet-washing (John 13:1-14). Notice verse 14. Jesus says, "Ye ought" to do it. This command has never been recalled in Scripture.

    3rd. The Lord's Supper, which is not to be "closed," but open to all saved people everywhere. As has been noted briefly, any minister can officiate in these ordinances, and no charges are to be made for these or any other services. God supplies our needs by freewill offerings of the people.

16. We believe in anointing the sick for healing, according to James 5:14-16. We do not believe in saved people using earthly means, such as doctoring, and using teas, etc., while these things may be useful to the unsaved, if God intended us to use them, he would certainly have mentioned it somewhere in his word. The only remedy we can find in the inspired Word is prayer and faith. While this has been hidden from us in the darkness of

apostasy, yet we believe Christ has lost none of his power to save, neither to heal (Heb. 13:8).

17. We do not believe in the use of tobacco (2 Cor. 7:1; Isa. 55:2).

18. We do not use opium, morphine, tea, or coffee, or any such narcotics, believing they are unnecessary, also injurious to our bodies; and we can use our means in a way that will more glorify God (1 Cor. 10:31).

19. We believe in dressing in modest apparel, and do not believe in the wearing of gold or pearls, etc. (1 Pet. 3:3; 1 Tim. 2:9).

20. We believe that women have the same right to preach, pray, etc., as men. (Acts 2:16-17). Also, Paul speaks of women who preached.

21. We believe in holding up holy hands when we sing or pray, etc., not as a mere form, but as the Spirit directs (1 Tim. 2:8; Ps. 134:2).

22. We believe in greeting each other with a holy kiss—men greeting men, and women greeting women—not necessarily every time we come together in meeting, but it is to be a kiss of love (Rom. 16:16; 1 Cor. 16:20; 1 Thess. 5:26).

23. We conduct prayer meeting, Sunday school, and family worship; but do not elect class leaders, superintendents, or any other officers. We believe in having family worship. It is a great blessing in a family, as many times impressions are made on the minds of the children in family worship which may result in their salvation. David and Daniel had worship three times a day (Ps. 55:17; Dan. 6:10). We believe also in secret prayer, which is indispensable to spirituality.

24. We believe that Christ will come to the world once more, and when he comes the dead, both righteous and wicked, will be resurrected and their final judgment pronounced (John 5:28-29). There are two resurrections: the first a spiritual resurrection from death in trespasses and sin to life in Christ; the second, a literal resurrection of all the dead, at which time the world will

be destroyed (2 Pet. 3:10). Much more might be said on this line, but for want of space we will close.

Dear reader, doubtless you have heard many reports as to this doctrine, and many of them not true. All we ask is a careful investigation of what we teach, also what we practice, and a careful study of the scriptures; and we feel sure God will convince you of the truth.

Characteristics
Of the True Church

by
Andrew L. Byers

Excerpted from *Birth of a Reformation,* by Andrew L. Byers (Anderson, Ind.: Gospel Trumpet Company, Copyright © 1921). Reprinted by Faith Publishing House, Guthrie, Okla.

THE TRUE church of God, comprising all Christians, has in her normal state under her divine head certain essential characteristics which make her exclusively the church, the whole and not a part. These might be expressed as follows:

1. Possession of divine spiritual life. If the church does not possess this she is not Christ's body and therefore not the church. She must know the Spirit of God.

2. Disposition to obey all Scripture and to let the Spirit have his way and rule. This constitutes her safety in matters of doctrine and government.

3. An attitude receptive to any further truth and light. This safeguards against dogmatism and a spirit of infallibil-

ity and intolerance, against interpreting Christianity in the light of traditions and old ideas.

4. Acknowledgment of good wherever found and the placing of no barrier that would exclude any who might be Christians. This makes salvation, a holy life, and a Christian spirit the only test of fellowship, and disapproves all human standards of church membership and fellowship.

We repeat that these constitute the scriptural standard of the church and characterize her in her unity and integrity. It is by lacking in one or more of these essentials that a sect is a sect. In the rise of the church out of apostasy any reformation that does not develop to the full the essentials that characterize the church in her wholeness and completeness must necessarily fall short of being the final reformation and must leave a cause for further reformation. This is the explanation of the existence of the so-called Christian sects, viewing them in the most charitable light. The Wesleys and their early associates sought for deeper personal spirituality as well as better spiritual association than was afforded in the state church of England. They brought to light and gave particular prominence to the doctrine of sanctification by faith and the witness of the Holy Spirit. Their work was a reform; but as in that day the question of division among Christians was not prominent, nor was the question of the one true Church understood or appreciated, their work took definite form in a body humanly organized and called Methodist. The Campbells had considerable light on the unity of the church, and proposed the Scriptures alone as a basis on which all Christians could unite. But they blindly shut themselves in on a point of doctrine by associating entrance into the kingdom or church with the act of immersion in such manner as to make a wall between them and other Christians who should give evidence of having received salvation and therefore church membership, otherwise than through baptism. Thus they made themselves a sect. John Winebrenner had the correct idea of the church as comprising all the saved, and his work was on an unsectarian basis. Lacking, however, in the quality of letting the

Spirit of God rule, eldership organizations were soon set up, a man rule came in, and they also became a sect. Inflexible as to doctrine, they closed the door of progress on themselves, rejected the truth on holiness, and became one of the most narrow of sects, though bearing the scriptural name, Church of God.

It must follow, and the assumption is already established, that a reformation which takes in full the characteristics defining the church in her wholeness must thereby reach the New Testament standard and therefore be the last, or final, reformation. No reformation can make good such claim if it does not proceed on whole-church lines or principles. If a reform does progress on those universal principles, we need look no farther for, nor await future years to reveal, the final reformation resulting in the restoration of all things to the Scriptural ideal.

The errors of the religious world are, and have been, the failure to so preach salvation truth that people may obtain and enjoy full deliverance from sin; failure to conform to the divine standard on all lines; the human ecclesiastical system, which hinders Holy Spirit organization and government; and separation of God's people into parties, thus making true church relation impossible. A movement that comprehends a correction of all these, and meets the scriptural standard, must therefore fill the measure of reform.

Reader, it is claimed for the movement represented in the teaching and labors of D. S. Warner, that it possesses these elements of finality, that by it God is bringing his people "out of all places where they have been scattered in the cloudy and dark day" of Protestant sectism, and is restoring Zion as at first. It is not assumed that Brother Warner was right on every point of doctrine or in every application of a scriptural text, but that the movement, in addition to being based on correct scriptural principles otherwise, possesses that flexibility and spirit of progress by which it adjusts itself as God gives light.

1. It teaches the scriptural process of salvation, by which people may obtain a real deliverance from sin and have the

Holy Spirit as a witness to their salvation.

2. The truth only, and obedience thereto, is its motto; and it recognizes the rule of the Holy Spirit in the organization and government of the church.

3. It does not assume to possess all the truth, but stands committed thereto, holding an open door to the entrance of any further light and truth.

4. The spirit of the movement is to acknowledge good wherever found and to regard no door into the church other than salvation and no test of fellowship other than true Christianity possessed within the heart.

Thus its basis is as narrow as the New Testament on the one hand, and as broad as the New Testament on the other. May it ever go forward on this line in the spread of the truth to all the world.

A Universal Posture
by
Albert F. Gray

Excerpted from the *Gospel Trumpet,* February 23, 1922.

THERE ARE several movements among Christian people, each claiming to be the one designed by God to supply the present need. While these movements hold some truths in common, and have contributed something toward the advance of the kingdom of God; yet, because of their differences, it would be hard to believe that all are designed of God to meet the present need: one may be, but certainly not all are. In thinking of these various movements, we think of them in the terms of their distinctive features. The mention of a particular body brings to the mind a particular doctrine or practice which is peculiar to that people, or to which they give special prominence. God's present movement must be so marked that it may be distinguished from all others. It is not the purpose of this article to attack any movement, nor to come to the defense of any particular body of people, but to point out these distinguishing marks.

A conscious effort to be distinct seems to have been made by some movements. Artificial means have been resorted to, such as a peculiar garb or a special form of salutation. It is evident that the present movement, which has for its object the unifying of all believers, can not hold arbitrary distinctions. It is not seeking differences, but seeking to remove them. In the sixteenth-century Reformation there were several bodies of reformed Christians, but no one of them was identical with the movement. It was bigger than any one of them. The present movement is not confined to sectarian limits and can not be defined in sectarian terms.

Bodies and movements among Christians are variously denominated. In some instances these names have come to be applied through circumstances, while in others they have been deliberately chosen. In all instances the names serve the same purpose—that of a distinguishing mark. The present movement differs from such bodies in that it accepts no sectarian name. It receives the Bible name— church of God—which it holds, not in a sectarian sense, but as the one name that is applicable to all Christians.

The preaching of doctrines previously neglected gave birth to most movements. In some instances these doctrines were neglected truths, while in others they were false doctrines. The people who rallied to these standards form the bodies which we usually think of in connection with these various doctrines. In this way even the truths of God's Book have been made to serve as means of division. The present movement differs in that it has no special doctrine. It seeks to unite all truth held by Christians and to ascribe to each the degree of prominence given it in the Bible. It does not claim to be the originator nor sole custodian of the truths that it holds, but accepts light as it is revealed and stands committed to the full truth.

Some denominations that are otherwise quite alike differ in form of organization. These forms range in variety from the imperialism of Rome to religious anarchy; yet they are alike in their nature in that they are of human origin. A defense of such organizations is sometimes made on the ground that they are needed to hold us together; but whatever holds a group of Christians together and at the same time holds them apart from other Christians, is to be condemned for dividing God's people. All this human ecclesiasticism stands in the way of God's present movement and must give place. The present movement is opposed to mere human government in spiritual affairs, of whatever sort it may be. It stands for the direct government of God through his Word and the Holy Spirit, and seeks to remove the human element in so far as it conflicts with such government, or hinders the unity of God's people. It makes no demands except those made in the gospel; it lays down no rules that are not necessarily binding upon all Christians; it makes no requirements that God does not make. In this it is fundamentally distinct from all sectarian institutions.

Besides regularly organized sects there are a few more recent movements that are seeking to maintain a nonsectarian position. Some such bodies oppose sectarian organization, acknowledge no creed but the Bible, and adhere to the Bible name. Yet they are marked by the special emphasis of some dogma, or a narrowness due to self-imposed conditions of fellowship, or by a spirit of self-righteous exclusiveness. The present movement differs from all such in its Christian universality: it acknowledges no such distinguishing features, but holds to those principles alone that identify it with primitive universal Christianity. This mark distinguishes it from all other movements and sects. Its name, its doctrine, its life, its government, and its fellowship are as universal as Christianity itself. Its name embraces all Christians; its teachings are applicable to all men; every Christian is amenable to its government;

and its fellowship is as broad as is the family of God.

But the present reformation is not only all-inclusive of the elements and principles of Christianity; but of necessity, it excludes all that is not essentially Christian. It has for its aim the unifying of all true Christians. Its method is to require all to accept all that is distinctively Christian and to renounce all that is not. It demands the rejection of all sectarian names and the acceptance of the name which the mouth of the Lord hath named. It calls for the renunciation of men's creeds and dogmas that all Christians may be free to believe and obey all of the Bible. It recognizes no fellowship save the "fellowship of the Spirit." It requires full submission to Holy Spirit government, and to no other. It aims at the destruction of all sectarian walls, that all Christians may be "one body in Christ." It is not responsible for division among God's people, but lays the charge against all who hold to their own distinguishing marks. It declares that any name, creed, or practice that does not rightfully belong to all Christians, but differentiates between them, has no part in this movement. It possesses and recognizes no mark that distinguishes Christians from Christians, or that differentiates between itself and universal Christianity; and in this it is distinct from all other movements.

Let us labor and pray that all Christians may so imbibe the spirit of God's present movement that we may become one as Christ and the Father are one that the world may believe.

Exploring the Doctrines
by
Frederick G. Smith

Excerpted from *Brief Sketch of the Origin, Growth, and Distinctive Doctrine of the Church of God Reformation Movement,* by F. G. Smith (Anderson, Ind.: Gospel Trumpet Company, 1927).

THE CHURCH OF GOD reformation movement was born in the midst of an intense revival of evangelical religion. A great holiness agitation was sweeping over the country. D. S. Warner and other pioneers saw that since genuine holiness can result only when the Spirit of God is given full control of the heart and life such complete surrender to the divine will must, under the direct leadership of the one Holy Spirit, ultimately result in a restoration of apostolic unity as well.

These pioneers were convinced beyond the shadow of a doubt that the long-neglected truths God was revealing to them demanded particular emphasis in these latter days, and to the promulgation of these truths they committed themselves unreservedly. The present-day movement is the result. And these same truths, as well as all other known truths, are still cherished and emphasized by us, and they form the real reason for our existence as a body of Christian people.

This reformation movement is not committed to ecclesiastical standards or doctrines repugnant to the human reason. We do not believe in extremism or fanaticism of any kind. We have no sympathy for strange or freak doctrines that are maintained only with subtle arguments or with forced and unnatural interpretations of Scripture. On the other hand we are convinced that, judged by the Word of God as the authoritative standard, the doctrinal position taken by the movement is fundamentally sound.

Doctrinally the movement may be classed as evangelical and orthodox. We believe the Bible teaches the Trinity, the inspiration and inerrancy of the Holy Scriptures, the deity of Christ, and the all-sufficiency of his sacrifice and atonement for sin, the office and work of the Holy Spirit, man's moral agency, and the supernaturalism of religious experience.

According to our understanding of the teaching of the Word of God, redemption is wrought in the heart of the individual believer by two definite works of divine grace, the first being termed *conversion* or regeneration, and the second *entire sanctification* or the baptism of the Holy Spirit.

The doctrine of divine healing and the possession and operation of spiritual gifts in general are strongly emphasized. We have witnessed many miraculous manifestations of the power of God in the healing of blindness, deafness, paralysis, cancer, tuberculosis, and practically all other diseases.

We believe in the immortality of the soul, in the Resurrection of the dead, the general Judgment, and in eternal rewards and punishments. We recognize three scriptural ordinances: baptism by immersion, the Lord's Supper, and foot washing. We recognize the Word of God as our only rule of faith and practice.

As a body we do not believe in participation in war, being convinced that this agelong pagan system is contrary to the teaching and Spirit of Jesus. We denounce secret orders of all kinds, and abstain from the use of all intoxicants and tobacco. We believe in a life of practical holiness and devotion to God.

The most distinctive doctrine taught by us is what we understand to be the true scriptural teaching concerning the church. According to the scriptural standard, we emphasize the doctrine of Christian unity and insist that true unity is to be found, not through hierarchies and apostolic successions and priestly corporations and church synods and ecclesiastical organizations and human creeds, but in the Christ alone, through spiritual attachment to and moral correspondence with him. Christian unity is essentially and primarily "in the Spirit." We hold sectarianism to be antiscriptural, and claim that sectarianism has resulted from two things in particular: (1) the teaching and practice of unscriptural doctrines, and (2) the substitution of the human for the divine in schemes of church organization and government. We regard every effort to organize the church of Christ humanly as being denominational and sectarian.

The Church of God reformation movement contends that the two fundamental principles of the primitive church— pure doctrine, and divine organization and government— were largely lost during the period of apostasy following the introduction of Christianity. During the undisputed reign of the Church of Rome the Word of God was supplanted by the doctrines, commandments, and traditions of men. And in place of that original concept of the church as made up of all spiritually regenerated believers whose only bond of union is their spiritual attachment to Christ through the Holy Ghost, the concept of the church that came to prevail was that of a humanly organized society patterned after the kingdoms of the world. Hence, in place of the *charismata* as the basis of spiritual organization and government, there developed an ecclesiastical corporation whose authority was altogether positional in character, patterned after the civil government of Rome.

The movement does not regard itself merely as a church among the churches, but as being different in character—a movement within the universal church, an unsectarian movement designed of God ultimately to affect the entire church and bring it to the realization of the grand scriptural ideal. We admit no other church name than scriptural titles, such as Church of God; still we often speak of the specific movement as "the reformation," and regard ourselves in our work as a sort of leaven diffusing itself through Christian society and the world, rather than as a geographically defined body of people seeking to build up another church with a denominational consciousness.

We hold with the Scriptures that the body of Christ is a spiritual organism, that the mode of induction into it is spiritual, and that the relationship of all the members of that body is fundamentally and essentially spiritual in character. The one requisite to spiritual unity and a practical inter-working of all the members of Christ, therefore, is an entire abandonment to the work and operations of the Holy Spirit in all ecclesiastical affairs. Such surrender to and leadership by the Holy Spirit is impossible under the sect system, where human ecclesiasticism reigns. To attain the high spiritual standard set forth in the New Testament requires the complete repudiation of the entire foreign system of human authority in church relationships and in spiritual operations.

When all the foreign systems are forsaken, when God's people return under the direction and inspiration of the Holy Spirit "to Zion with songs and everlasting joy upon their heads"—when the principle of the theocracy as originally instituted in Zion is again recognized as the only ecclesiastical organization and government for the people of God—then, thank God, the sweet spirit of unity from heaven flows through and through all the sanctified hearts cleansed from sinful, carnal elements, and binds them all together with ties of holy love and fellowship.

Such, in brief, is the goal of this reformation. We regard it as a concrete expression of God's effort in our day to cure the evils of sectarianism and to bring about that complete and perfect unity among Christians for which Christ prayed. From its beginning this movement has not centered in nor has it been dependent for its life and success upon any man or set of men. Christ has been and still is its true center of attraction and source of authority, and loyalty to all the truth of God is its inspiring motive.

Heart Talks
On the Church
by
Charles W. Naylor

Excerpted from the *Gospel Trumpet,* February 28, 1929.

WHEN we speak of the Church of God we do not or should not mean merely this movement. This movement is merely a part of the church. The church is made up of all Christians everywhere and all Christians are in the same church we are in. Christians in general recognize this. At the same time they overlook some very important things concerning the church. As one brother said, "The church is not as a lumber pile, it is like a building. It is joined together, knit together and framed together for a habitation of God through the Spirit." So Christian people must be in a cooperative relation to properly represent the church. It is for this reason that we teach that Christians should come out of denominations and unite together on the basis of their union with Christ.

Now about the question of denominationalism. When Paul went into a city and preached and the people got saved and a church was raised up did he form a denomination? No, this church was just like the other churches that had been raised up by Paul and the other apostles elsewhere. God was the head of each one of them and the Lord of each one of them and of all of them together. They were not divided into denominations. When a division arose among them the apostles were quick to condemn it and to demand unity. When man rule began to raise its head they were ready to act against it. When we preach and raise up a congregation we do just like Paul did. We establish a congregation of the church of God, the same church of which Paul established congregations. We establish congregations just like he established and if his congregations were not denominational are the congregations that we establish denominational? Certainly they are not if they maintain the attitude and relation that was maintained in the early churches and this is the very goal of our endeavor.

In the denominational churches people join whether they are saved or unsaved. Their names are put down on the church roll. They are members of the church no matter what they do. Among us membership is on a different basis. We recognize the fact that a man has no right to membership in a local congregation unless he is a child of God. It takes real salvation to make him fit to be a member or to give him the ability to function as a member of the church. Membership among us therefore is on a different basis than it is in denominationalism. In some of the denominations the local congregation, as the smallest unit, with other congregations, goes to make up a unit having greater authority than the single congregation and having officials of greater authority than those in the local congregation. Then over these greater units there is a greater control generally speaking, and this greater control when traced up centers in one man or a number of men, in a pope, a general conference, a synod, a yearly meeting or the like. This official or this official body is the ultimate authority in the organization. There is no appeal to a higher power except it be an individual appeal to God.

With us the local church is at the same time the greatest and the smallest unit. The local church stands by itself as the most important factor in our work locally and whatever power there may be above that is only the power of God in the individual joined with the same power in other individuals giving them collectively a divine authority but not partaking in any sense of a human authority.

We recognize no law-making body, nor man-made ecclesiastical laws. We recognize no humanly bestowed authority in the general church. There is no one in the place of God for us, but where there is a human ecclesiastical organization that organization stands in the place of God to the people. Its authority is a usurped authority. When one is a Christian and belongs to a denomination he belongs to two churches, the church of God and the church of man. Belonging to the latter we deem an unnecessary thing. What we stand for is for churches like Paul and John and Peter and the other apostles established, having the same relation to each other that they had and having the same divinely empowered ministers. When one gets a good view of the true church of God, membership in a humanly devised church does not appeal to him. It will not take the place of the divine church.

Many people do not understand why we emphasize the church so much, but one clear look at the beauty of the divine forever spoils one for the humanly devised system. The denominational authority being a human authority, humanly given, is ecclesiastical tyranny from which once freed we would not again submit to. To be sure freedom does not mean license or freedom from government. It means discipline of self and discipline by God's ministers. It means submission one to another and to God. We cannot make people see the spiritual evils of denominationalism until they see God's plan and God's church. When they see these they see the other by contrast. The name church of Christ is just the same as church of God, for Christ is God.

When we call people out of denominationalism we are proselyters only if we do it in a sectarian way. If we call them out of the false to the true that is not proselyting. If we merely call them out of one body into another of a similar kind that is proselytism. We should avoid anything of this sort. People who see the Zion of God come to it with rejoicing and have reason to forever be thankful for the true way of God which every child of God ought gladly to embrace.

The Difference Is Fundamental

by
Charles E. Byers

Reprinted from a tract by the same title, published by the Gospel Trumpet Company in 1947.

OFTEN the question is asked, "What is the difference between the Church of God and other churches?" Others say, "I cannot see any difference between the Church of God and other churches." It is true that, while the difference is fundamental, it is unseen, for the fundamental difference is mostly spiritual and not physical. The Church of God in many of her activities differs little from other religious bodies. She owns church houses, has her Seminary and College, a publishing house, missionary board and missionaries, a church extension board and other boards, conducts Sunday schools, church services, revivals, camp meetings, and her members preach, pray, sing, and play musical instruments, and she conducts her worship in many respects just as other orthodox religious bodies do.

While the Church of God is fundamentally different from all other churches in many respects, however in this article we wish to speak of only one fundamental difference—that of her fellowship. John, writing to the members of the church of God of the first century, said, "Truly our fellowship is with the Father and with his Son Jesus Christ. The life . . . we have seen and heard declare we unto you, that ye may also have fellowship with us." Being in Christ was the primary cause for the fellowship which existed among the early Christians and in the church of God. Their fellowship rested not in an organization, a doctrine, a creed, or in the embracing of certain principles passed on and approved by the apostles or by any other body of men or religious leaders. Their fellowship rested in the receiving of Jesus Christ as being the Son of God, the Messiah.

John, referring to himself and to the other apostles who constituted the ministry of the church of God, said, "Truly our fellowship is with the Father, and with his Son Jesus Christ." He then declares that if we would have fellowship with them we must believe in and accept Jesus Christ as the Son of God, for in him only is found the source of Christian fellowship. In verse 6 of this first chapter of the first epistle of John he says, "If we say that we have fellowship with him [Christ], and walk in darkness [commit sin], we lie, and do not the the truth." In verse 9 he says, "If we confess our sins, he [Christ] is faithful and just to forgive us our sins and to cleanse us from all unrighteousness." Then in verse 7 he says, "If we walk in the light [truth and holiness] as he [Christ] is in the light, we have fellowship one with another, and the blood of Jesus Christ his Son cleanseth us from all sin."

Thus the church of God in her fellowship is fundamentally different, for her fellowship embraces only those who have been saved from their sins through the shed blood of Jesus Christ, the Son of God. While the Church of God is made up only of those who have been cleansed from their sins, yet unlike any other religious organization or church, she embraces and extends the right hand of fellowship to every blood-washed soul under heaven, regardless of race, color, nationality, or creed. For if we have been saved from our sins through Christ and walk in the light as he is in the light, we have fellowship one with the other.

Today we have in Christendom many sects, divisions, and clans called churches. In these different organizations are many of God's own dear children who have been saved through the blood of Christ. Yet they cannot all sit at the one holy communion table of the Lord and fellowship together because the organization which they have joined forbids their communing with those who do not hold membership in their religious body. The reason for this lies in the fact that something other than being saved in Jesus Christ constitutes their fellowship. It rests in a certain creed, doctrine, or in some human tradition bound upon them by their religious leaders. There is only one requirement for fellowship in the Church of God—being washed from our sins in the blood of Jesus Christ.

One may be saved from his sins, yet believe in some unscriptural doctrine; he may have been unscripturally baptized, being in ignorance of the true mode; he may lack understanding in many of the doctrines of Christ; yet if he is truly converted, born again, if he has been saved from his sins by faith in Christ, he may have and does have fellowship with all of God's people in the Church of God.

The communion table of the Church of God is spread not only for those who understand the doctrines of Chirst perfectly, as taught in the Word of God, or for those who belong to a particular sect or embrace certain teaching passed upon by a group of ministers or elected leaders, but for every soul that knows Jesus Christ in the pardon of sins. Any communion table that does not invite to it all those saved in any community is not the communion table of the Lord Jesus Christ, for he is not the Savior of a particular nation, race, or clan, but he is the Savior of all men.

Thus the Church of God is fundamentally different from all other churches and religious bodies, because she refuses to acknowledge any sect, creed, or cause for Christian fellowship other than that spoken of by John—being in Christ. Blessed will be the day for the cause of Christ when every child of God will ignore the doctrines and creeds of men, which hinder true Christian fellowship and divide the body of Christ into the many sects that now exist. Let us do as Paul exhorted the Christians at Corinth, "Wherefore come out from among them, and be ye separate, saith the Lord, and touch not the unclean thing; and I will receive you" (2 Cor. 6:17).

Reformation Principles
by
Albert J. Kempin

Excerpted from the *Gospel Trumpet,* November 1, 1952.

WE, with all evangelical Christians, say that saints are made through the precious blood of Christ and not by canonization. We stress the priesthood of believers and uphold the prophetic function of the New Testament ministry.

We take our stand with the saints and reformers of the past and present against liturgical, sacerdotal, ceremonial trends in Christianity and contend earnestly for heartfelt, experiential, spiritual worship and for the centrality of God's Word in our houses of worship.

We say that the redeemed heart is the sanctuary of God. Redeemed people are the habitation of God through the Holy Spirit. Truth is the light that lights the candles of worship, and holiness adorns and beautifies God's house, which we are.

Candles, vestments, priestly ministration, holy things and places belong to the old order rather than to the new order which Christ came to establish. They belong to the legal dispensation rather than to the gospel dispensation.

Through the reformation begun by Christ and continued by holy men who were moved by the Holy Spirit, we attempt to break the centralization and domination of ecclesiasticism and restore the Word of God to its rightful place in the church as its creed and discipline.

We restore the truth on the lordship of Christ and say he now sits upon the throne and reigns as King of kings and Lord of lords. All enemies are now being subjected to him through the preaching of his gospel. The last enemy to be conquered and destroyed is death. Satan's power is now broken and sin's dominion gone. All who wish may reign in life by and through the Lord Jesus Christ.

The reformation movement attempts to continue God's new order in this world by removing the creeds of men, breaking down the walls of sectarianism, and leading believers into the blessed unity found in Christ where natural birth, social distinction, education, and mere morality have no standing or recognition.

To one and all the appeal is, "Ye must be born again." Water baptism, church joining, resolutions, education, cannot bring salvation to anyone. Only faith in the shed blood of Christ can cleanse the guilty, confessing, repenting soul from all sin. Such persons are one in Christ. "By one Spirit are we all baptized into one body."

We say to sinner and saint alike, Christ alone takes in the members of the church, which is his body, and that by being converted. Christian experience makes us members of the church of God. Salvation is the only door of entrance into the church.

We hold no Lord but Christ and no creed but the Bible. It is still the sinner's guide to Christ and the saint's food. No other guide or discipline is needed.

We stress leadership without lordship, because we are all brethren and Christ is Lord and Master. We preach the kingdom of God without a carnal, earthly millennium on earth. We hold up the banner of Christian unity and not merely church union.

We preach and practice holiness without self-righteousness, spirituality without fanaticism, education without formalism, beauty in worship without pomp and show.

We have "interest centers" but not worship centers, because the center of our worship is Christ himself whom no picture, no candles, no gilded altars can properly represent or enhance. He must be seen with the eyes of our understanding, else we do not see him at all.

Let us share these reformation principles with all men. They have set us free. They will bring glorious liberty to all who embrace them. You can help the Lord Jesus to carry on his work of reformation through your redeemed life and by your Christian testimony. Thus we usher in God's new order in this present world.

Together with All True Christians

by
John D. Crose

Written by Dr. Crose in 1955 as an open letter to other missionaries in Korea.

WITH SINCERITY and humility we recognize the splendid, spiritual work and real sacrificial service rendered by the many missionaries and Korean churches in trying to win this country to Christ. As missionaries using the scriptural name, Church of God, we prayerfully desire to live worthy of this great name, and as well, encourage a spiritually united Christian fellowship and co-operation in harmony with our Lord's farewell prayer (John 17:6-23). Without apology, we believe the whole church belongs to God and not to any one denomination, and for this reason we desire to be identified with the whole family of God—i.e. the whole Church of God as declared in Ephesians 3:14-15.

Whatever we may be able to do here in Korea—as a non-sectarian, international mission—we certainly wish to help, and not hinder, what is already being well done in declaring the basic, saving truth of the Gospel to the people of this unfortunate land. In this unique and vital undertaking, the *real success of one* truly becomes the *success of all*.

A Time to Remember: TEACHINGS

Second in importance to that of our evangelizing the world, the pointed slogan of the Christian Brotherhood Hour radio program has meaning, that is, "A United Church in a Divided World." In fairness to all Christian groups, this can only come about through a dynamic, spiritual fellowship among ALL of God's true people *capable of neutralizing* all antagonistic denominational differences between us. This is imperative now, so our world can believe, and with conviction accept the Bible message and experience.

It is our avowed purpose to become *no more* than a spiritually balanced movement within the divided church; teaching and living the central truths of the New Testament as generally believed and practiced by most evangelical Christians. "Endeavoring to keep the *unity of the Spirit* in the bond of peace (Eph. 4:1-4) till we all come in the *unity of the faith* and of the knowledge of the Son of God" (Eph. 4:13), holding to Christ as the supreme head of the Church. We do *not* profess to have all of the answers to the church's problems, or understand all of the mysteries of the Scriptures, but we do believe there is enough *known* truth, if obeyed, to save a lost world and unite God's people in a working fellowship if only we ministers will faithfully preach these basic truths in Christian courtesy and love (2 Timothy 3:15-17).

To make the above position realistic and applicable to the needs of our time, we refuse to set up human creed barriers, denominational standards of our own, or any other boundaries to separate ourselves from other real Christians, who are in fact as much a part of the whole church as we are. We desire to emphasize as essential and vital only those well-known principles conducive to the saving of a lost world and the unifying of all regenerated believers into a spiritual fellowship and communion in Christ. We are persuaded that the "new spiritual birth" is the only valid induction into the family of God, since Jesus said, "Ye *must* be born from above," to even see the Kingdom of God. And when a convert to *Christ* requests baptism we should try to make it crystal-clear that baptism signifies his testimony of a personal experience of salvation and that he is entitled to an unlimited fellowship in the *whole* universal Church of God.

Whatever material organization or agency we may use in evangelizing the world, and in establishing the local group fellowship, or church (not denomination), such organization must never be permitted to divide God's people or disfigure "The Church Beautiful" for which Christ died. Building contractors quickly tear down the scaffolding, however effective it was during the building operations, so the beauty of the building may be clearly seen by all; just so, we must soon eliminate all human obstructions that hinder the glorious revelation and view of the universal church of God that cost Christ his life's blood (Acts 20:28). In the meantime, this movement using the name, Church of God, claims *no exclusive right* to this universal name of the whole church, and more, does not regard itself as a "denomination among other denominations," but simply a reformation within the divided church. Though we take no membership, in the common and denominational way, we do press the divine claims of the Gospel for a very definite decision for and conversion to Christ, and literally consider every congregation thus raised as a part of the whole Church of God as mentioned in Revelation 7:9-17—including all "blood-washed" saints of all ages.

It is with the above convictions and principles that, as a non-sectarian board, The Church of God Missionary Board, 1303 East Fifth Street, Anderson, Indiana, operates throughout the whole world. With most all of our leading Christian churchmen calling for a united church fellowship, in our desperately divided world, there certainly can be no serious objection to our trying honestly to be non-sectarian even in the midst of the present sectarian setup of our present denominational world. When such men of God as Billy Graham, E. Stanley Jones, Leslie Weatherhead, Nels F. Ferre, Karl Barth, Paul C. Payne, J. C. Ryle of Liverpool, Henry Knox Sherrill, Dale Oldham, together with many others of deep spiritual insight and influence, plainly declare the wrong of our divisions and even believe that such divisions actually hinder revival in the churches, as well as retard the evangelization of our sinful world, then surely every Christian should seek the Bible way back to a universal fellowship in Christ so as to neutralize our sectarian differences.

It is reasonable to believe that *surely one does not have to be sectarian* in order to be a Christian in the New Testament sense of the term. To the contrary, every true Christian may become a potential factor, capable of creating the real unity of spirit that Christ prayed for, simply by practicing brotherly love towards other fellow Christians and ignoring all denominational barriers that would otherwise divide them in spirit. With like spiritual experiences, the early, first-century martyrs declared their faith and fidelity to each other with an undying affection thus, *"Who shall separate us* from the love of Christ?" rather than, Who shall unite us? They became automatically one by virtue of their like experiences in Christ and manifested true Christian courtesy to maintain that oneness. The separation of spiritual fellowship from organizational and denominational control may become as important as the separation of the church from the state.

And finally, we believe and affirm that the New Testament declaration on the unity of God, together with all of his people, remains valid today in these words: There is one God and father of us all—one Lord and one mediator between God and man—one faith—one baptism—one hope of eternal life—one fold and one shepherd—one door into the sheepfold—one body, the church—one spirit by which we have access to the Father—one head to the church, even Christ, and it still is possible for God to set the members in the body as it pleases him, daily adding to the church those that are being saved. To this declaration for the *whole church,* we dedicate ourselves, together with all other true Christians in all the world, so multitudes might be saved and the divided church made one in spirit now.

This We Believe
by
R. Eugene Sterner

Reprinted from *Vital Christianity,* June 11, 1972.

THIS MOVEMENT started around 1880, initially under the leadership of Daniel Sidney Warner and a few associates. It has spread until now there are nearly twenty-five hundred congregations in the United States and Canada and well over one thousand congregations in other countries. It is not large as compared with some other church bodies, of course, but we think it has a significant message. The original concept which Warner felt so important was the uniting of the scriptural concept of holiness with the equally scriptural concept of Christian unity. He felt that on no other basis could true unity be realized except in the power and presence of the Holy Spirit. This was of prime importance since Jesus linked the effectiveness of his followers in the world to their unity in a loving fellowship. "By this all men will know that you are my disciples," he said, "if you have love for one another" (John 13:35). He prayed for his disciples saying, "I do not pray for these only, but also for those who believe in me through their word, that they may all be one; even as thou, Father, art in me, and I in thee, that they also may be in us, so that the world may believe that thou hast sent me" (John 17:20-21). You see Jesus felt that our Christian witness depended upon our unity. That's why unity is so important.

Thus a good many years before we heard much about unity among the denominations, and long before the present "ecumenical movement," Warner and others were preaching vigorously the unity of God's people on the basis of vital personal experience in Christ.

A Time to Remember: TEACHINGS

Basic in all this was the fact that the Word of God was taken seriously. We believe in the authority of the Scriptures and in the divine inspiration of those sacred writings. This movement thus took its place in the mainstream of conservative, evangelical theology. The purpose was not to start another denomination but simply to be open to all God's people wherever they might be and to keep open to the wholeness of scriptural truth. A written creed seemed to be out of order. It seemed to crystallize thinking and arrest growth, instead of stimulating a growing understanding of the Scriptures. Since the Bible speaks of only one church—one fellowship of all God's people—it seemed right to take a stand of openness to all Christians everywhere. So they took the stance of openness on the Godward side to all the truth they could learn and openness on the manward side to fellowship with all Christians. The church, therefore, was seen not as a denomination, but as a fellowship in Christ which embraces all who are in him.

It is for that reason that we, as a people, have never accepted formal church joining. We recall that in the early days of Christianity, the fellowship was made up of an inspired people with inspired leaders, and with an inspired kind of membership. Act 2:47 describes those people as "Praising God and having favor with all the people. And the Lord added to their number day by day those who were being saved." They were made members of that body as they were converted to Christ. Being a member of the church then was more like being a member of your parental family. It came about by spiritual birth, or as Jesus put it, by being "born again." So you see, with us membership is based upon fellowship in Christ.

That puts vital personal experience with Christ at the very center of our life together. When the Apostle Paul wrote to the Ephesians, he said, "And you he made alive, when you were dead through the trespasses and sins in which you once walked. . . ." Then he added, "God, who is rich in mercy, out of the great love with which he loved us, even when we were dead through our trespasses, made us alive together with Christ . . . and raised us up with him . . ." (Eph. 2:1, 4-6). That chapter closes with these words, "In whom you also are built into it for a dwelling place of God in the Spirit" (v. 22). There you have it. Christ finds us lost in sin, but he "quickens" us and raises us up to find a fellowship together in which he himself lives and works. From bondage to freedom, from separateness and alienation to fellowship, from captivity to creativity! At the threshhold of the fellowship is the personal encounter with Christ. Fellowship in the church is the result of personal spiritual renewal.

And it is more than mere fellowship on the human level. The presence of the living Christ is what gives the fellowship meaning and character. That makes it something holy. It is the presence of Christ that makes it so, for whatever he dwells in, that becomes holy. That's the meaning of holiness in the Bible. Nothing was holy of itself—even the temple of the Old Testament days. It was holy only because of the presence of the Lord—the Shekinah.

Now this has special meaning when you recall the promise made by Jesus to his followers. "Again I say to you, if two of you agree on earth about anything they ask, it will be done for them by my Father in heaven. For where two or three are gathered in my name, there am I in the midst of them" (Matt. 18:19-20). Then the genius of it all is in the presence and power of Christ? Yes! The church is more than an organization or institution. It is a living fellowship. The New Testament speaks of the church as the "body of Christ," that is to say the body of believers who are obedient in carrying forward his mission in the world. The church is to be *the people of God on mission*. And, according to the Colossian letter (1:18), "He [Christ] is the head of the body, the church." As his followers, we are to be united in obedience. It is not unity for the sake of unity, it is unity in *purpose* and *function*.

It is that concept of the church that we try to keep in view. Being human and subject to all human limitations, we cannot claim to have fully expressed that ideal, but it does represent our basic stance. If it seems pretentious, perhaps a little further explanation will help.

A fellow minister of another group, a warm friend of mine, once asked me how we could claim the name Church of God. ''Isn't it pretty bold,'' he asked me, ''to claim such a name that refers to the universal church?'' My answer was that no one in his right mind would claim that we were the whole church—all Christians—but that, as Paul the Apostle wrote to different congregations as to the church of God in that place, so it can be, and is, today. He referred simply to the local fellowship as a part of the total fellowship. If a local congregation is universal in spirit and open in fellowship to all, it can very properly be called by that biblical name. If, however, any group becomes sectarian or ingrown in spirit, it denies the name and brings shame upon it. I have often quoted my good friend, Dr. Gene Newberry, who said, ''We dare not lay claim upon the name Church of God in a sectarian sense. We lay claim to that name as a sailor lays claim to the great wide sea.'' I might add that the sea doesn't belong to the sailor. The sailor belongs to the sea. And the universal church of God does not belong to the group of which I am gladly a part. We belong to the church of God, and so far as we are concerned there is no barrier between us and any committed Chrisitan any place. Our hearts are open to you. We feel that if a person belongs to Jesus Christ, he belongs to all those who belong to Jesus Christ. Doesn't the scripture say that ''We are members one of another?'' (Eph. 4:25). Don't take that lightly.

You can easily see why we cannot accept the mere merging of denominations or the federation of denominations as authentic biblical unity. Whatever values such mergers or federations may have for cooperative work, we must in all honesty distinguish between that and the unity of the Spirit. We must also add, that such moves may or may not involve the unity of the spirit. But the two are not the same.

The Christian Brotherhood Hour seeks to express this spirit to the world. It is not a sectarian program. It is provided by our fellowship as a loving service to all, though our listening friends do help us in the purchase of air time on stations abroad. We are very grateful for that help and I assure you it is used as a service to all.

It gives me a special joy to speak on behalf of my colleagues and friends. They would not all agree with me on every point but, in the main, I believe I can represent their basic convictions. Perhaps you, my friend, do not agree with me at every point, but we can have fellowship in Christ. One of our early writers put it this way:

We reach our hands in fellowship
To every blood-washed one,
While love entwines about each heart
In which God's will is done.

—Charles W. Naylor

Just Who Are We?

by
Kenneth F. Hall

Reprinted from *Vital Christianity,* January 2, 1977.

WE ARE friendly folks. We worship together, pray together, work together right here in your community. We're just average people, trying to raise our families and pay our debts and make ends meet and be good Christians. We like to have new faces in our congregation, and we like to see those new faces come back again and again. Our church doors are open to you.

A Time to Remember: TEACHINGS

The name out front labels our place of worship as a "Church of God." Now that may just add to your confusion, because there are a lot of church buildings around with all kinds of names. There are reasons for these names. So what is the reason for our use of the name "Church of God"?

We go by this name because we find that term often applied to the early church in the New Testament. We like to get as close as we can to those early days and the teachings of Christ.

But "Church of God" has other meanings for us. To us the term can apply to all Christians who have given their lives to Christ. By using that name we want to identify ourselves with all born-again Christians, no matter what barriers some of them may raise among themselves. We use the name, because we want to witness that we are a part of the one church which Christ founded.

As you have already read, one thing we think very important is the unity of all of God's children in the one church which Jesus Christ established through his ministry long ago. We try to put that belief into practice in various ways. One way is by recognizing every person who shows that he or she has a real Christian experience as an actual member of our group. Thus we have no formal church membership. You become a member of the body of Christ by accepting his salvation.

Of course there are other convictions that hold Church of God people together. We place a great deal of emphasis upon the Bible, and when people ask us about our creed we often just point at the Bible and say that there it is. Each person studies the Bible, meditates upon it, makes use of the best advice available about it, looks to the Holy Spirit—it's remarkable how closely we all come out together. The Bible describes the way of salvation, and so we stress evangelism a great deal.

In the end your beliefs count most when they are lived out. There are no hypocrites who are really in the Church of God, for by our definition of church membership only genuine Christians belong. Church of God folks try to live the highest possible kind of life—high ethically, morally, and spiritually. Of course, we don't expect to do it all in our own power, for we lean heavily upon the cleansing and empowering work of the Holy Spirit to sustain us.

We simply try to live by the Bible and the guidance of God and back our actions with the love of Christ.

This congregation tries to carry on its work and its business affairs under the guidance of the Holy Spirit with dignity and yet with enthusiasm. We think the church has an educational as well as an evangelistic task, and so we carry on Sunday school classes, youth meetings, and many other local activities. We meet for worship, for praise, for prayer, and for fellowship. We serve in the community.

We also have Christian interests beyond our local boundaries, and thus we join with sister congregations across the country in carrying on overseas mission work and assisting churches in more than twenty countries, in sponsoring church colleges, in publishing Christian literature, in caring for our aging ministers, in promoting Christian education, in broadcasting the gospel worldwide, in extending our work into new communities and among underprivileged people right here in North America. We are concerned with emergency help and disaster wherever it occurs. Our general offices are located in Anderson, Indiana.

We are a fast-growing group of earnest Christians. We invite you to worship with us.

From the Editor's Pen

by
Harold L. Phillips

Reprinted from *Vital Christianity*, July 31, 1977.

Bible Content
In essence the Bible is the story of salvation. This theme dominates its pages from Genesis to Revelation, the first book to the last. It sets forth God's saving purpose and saving acts on behalf of his people, the whole human race. It depicts man in a predicament from which only the gracious mercy of a loving God can rescue him.—"Operation Rescue," February 28, 1965

Bible Inspiration
God's Spirit was active in the writing of the Scriptures. At the same time they came to us through human instrumentality. This dual relationship of the divine and the human is affirmed in one of the New Testament epistles by the statement that "men moved by the Holy Spirit spoke from God" (2 Pet. 1:21).—"Knowing God Through the Bible," October 22, 1967

Bible Interpretation
A good principle of biblical interpretation is to go to the plain and unmistakable passages first and formulate your basic conceptions of truth. Then turn to the more perplexing sections and use your basic principles as guides. Or, for that matter, with basic conceptions settled you can leave some of the finer points of interpretation to the specialists who will still be wrestling with them millenniums hence.— "The Answer is No," August 1, 1959

Christi

. . . If we believe and set forth a full-orbed message about Christ, emphasizing the teachings of the New Testament concerning him, we will come to grips with much larger areas of doctrine than just pious generalizations about a Galilean carpenter. We must reckon with *who he claimed to be, what he actually did,* and *why he did it.* When we do this, we will find ourselves stressing Christ as the divine Son of God, the Savior of sinners, the sanctifier of believers, the healer of the sick, the head of the church which he purchased with his own blood.—"When Christ Is Made Central," September 8, 1951

Christian Life

Salty Christians—that's what we need today, Christians whose lives make a difference wherever they go and whatever they do, every day of the week. The world is sick of sticky, flat, tasteless, joyless, it-really-doesn't-make-any-difference-in-my-life Christianity.

Rightly understood, the whole church (not just the ministerial staff) is "called" and "sent." We are called to repentance, to dedication, to renewal, to worship, to training. We are sent out into the world to witness by both word and deed, to *be salt* out in the thick of life and its problems. A little veneer of Sunday morning piety has no right to call itself "Christian" in any meaningful sense.—"The Christian as Salt," May 16, 1965

Church Membership

. . . The New Testament church could not be "joined" in today's sense of that term. In the New Testament sense the church is God's family and its members are "born" into it by spiritual birth. It is God, and not man, who sets us in the body of Christ, the real and only church.—"More Members—Less Attendance," November 21, 1965

Church Name

Obviously, we have no patent on the name, "Church of

God." We use it not because we have any notion that we are the only Christians in the world, but simply because it is the most-often used designation for the church in the New Testament, and because we abhor both denominational and sectarian terminology in reference to the body of Christ.— "No Patent on the Name," December 15, 1951

Death

The ultimate hope of the Christian lies beyond death and the grave. He rests confidently in the promises of God for eternal life. In a sense, death may seem grim and terrible, but it can be managed well as the last great crisis of this life by those who believe that as we set our feet in the waters of that dark and mysterious river we cross to the other side with our hand in the hand of our Lord and Master.—"The Face of Grief and Death," March 7, 1965

Healing

We do not accept the idea that miracles ceased with the apostolic age. We do not believe that healing grace ended with the Book of Acts. . . . We believe that God's redemptive plan includes the whole man, that he made provision not only to save our souls, but also to heal our bodies, to deliver us eventually even from the sting of death and the corruption of the body through the resurrected life.— "What Holds Us Together?" October 16, 1954

Prayer

. . . God is a prayer-hearing and prayer-answering God even though we may not altogether understand all of his will or ways. To settle for less than this is to rob ourselves of some of the most precious experiences a human being can have, the conviction and consciousness that in a given set of circumstances his own prayer was heard and answered, and that God does at times intervene in the circumstances of our lives and needs.—"Some Convictions about Prayer," February 18, 1973

Revelation

God's method of revelation is a progressive one. More light is shed on our path as we step forward in what we have already been given. Truth, understanding, and insight are not given to us all neatly wrapped in a package and tied with a bow.—"The Holy Spirit at Work in the Church," July 21, 1962

Salvation

There is value in pursuing the study of the meaning of the atonement and the typical steps to salvation. But it is also possible to make these too complex and too rigid. Let's not forget the crux—God giving in love and man reaching out in hunger and need. When these are present, something new is born, grace is given, guilt burdens are lifted, and the joy of a new relationship surges in the heart.—"The Crux of the Good News," September 30, 1973

Sanctification

We are convinced that we stand on biblical ground in believing that it is the purpose, the power, and the provision of Christ through the Holy Spirit that believers should be delivered *in this life* from willful transgression against the known law and will of God. We interpret Romans 7 as being descriptive of Paul's pre-christian experience. Therefore we can question with Paul, "Shall we continue in sin?" and echo his answer, "God forbid. How shall we, that are dead to sin, live any longer therein?" (Rom. 6:1-2).—"What Holds Us Together?" October 16, 1954

Sectism

. . . Sectarians are finding it harder and harder to keep people fenced away from their brothers and sisters in Christ. Christians all around the world are looking askance at the sectarian iron curtains. They are shamed by them; they long to see them torn away; they are striving to leap over them to find fellowship with the rest of God's people. They are calling upon others who can see this vision of the true church, the body and bride of Christ, to "come out" from behind the iron curtain of sectarian affiliation to find freedom and fellowship among God's people.—"Getting Behind the Iron Curtains (III)," September 27, 1952

"Tongues"

This "tongues-evidence" theory [of the presence of the Holy Spirit] we have always rejected as a combination of extremism and biblical misinterpretation. In fact, our fathers of long years ago were so unalterably opposed to this sort of thing that they asserted freely that the gibberish that so often accompanies this type of emphasis was in reality of the devil and should be shunned as a dangerous delusion.

In this generation we have not often stated our objections in this same language, but our aversion to this heresy has not changed.—"Information and Misinformation," April 18, 1959

Unity

Christian unity at the deepest level is the fruit of the workings of the Holy Spirit in the hearts and lives of Christian believers. It is a recognition of a kinship created by the grace of God. In this sense it is more the work of God than the work of men.

Men can and should find ways of expressing the unity which they experience in Christ. But it is necessary to remind ourselves from time to time that the essence of unity is relationship in Christian experience, which in turn is a gift given only to the penitent and the obedient.—"Christian Unity and the Fruit of the Holy Spirit," May 16, 1959

The Secret of Salvation

by
Enoch E. Byrum

Excerpted from *The Secret of Salvation*, by E. E. Byrum
(Grand Junction, Mich.: Gospel Trumpet Company, 1896).

GOD did not make man to be lost. It is his will that all
should be saved with an everlasting salvation. Man was not
placed here in this world in a sinful state, but was created in
the likeness of God (Gen. 1:26), pure and holy, on a plane
with his Maker, and could walk and talk with him. This was
indeed a blessed privilege. Not only was this the case, but
he had the promise that he could remain in that relation as
long as he did not disobey God. He was, however, told the
penalty of disobedience; nevertheless he yielded to the
voice of the serpent, through whose subtlety and cunning
devices, plans were laid to cause the curse of sin to be
brought upon mankind through disobedience to God.

Now began their life under the curse of sin. While they
had been created in the likeness of God, now since their fall
their children inherited the same fallen nature as themselves
(Gen. 5:3), and this is the inbred, sinful nature that has
passed upon all men since that time. The seed of sin having
been planted in the hearts of our foreparents is our inheritance from them.

To have full salvation is to be redeemed from all sin, and to be redeemed is to be brought back into the first state. Before the fall of man he was pure and holy, and Eden was not stained with the guilt of sin; but now since sin has passed upon all men, is it possible for such sin-benighted souls to reach the same plane of purity and holiness while here in this life as was enjoyed in Eden? Truly it is possible, else the plan of redemption is a failure.

As redemption means restoring to the first or original condition, then truly it is the mission of our Redeemer to bring about such a state of affairs. Through the plan of salvation provisions have been made wherein God will deal justly with all men, and in his infinite wisdom he knows exactly how to dispose of humanity, and it matters not to us if we can not fully understand just how he will deal with the people of past ages, throughout eternity. Let that be as it may, we are living in a gospel dispensation and will be judged by the Word of God given for us.

God is the author of this salvation. David says: He that is our God is the God of salvation; and daily loadeth us with his benefits (Ps. 68: 19-20). It cometh down from heaven as freely as the water from an ever-flowing fountain, and is offered without money and without price. Yet it was purchased for us at a very great price.

As God looked upon the sin-cursed world and beheld the awful wickedness, the tender chords of love and mercy moved him to sacrifice the brightest gem of glory for the sins of the world, and give his only begotten Son as a Redeemer for all who would believe on him and turn from their sins. What a price! This loving Son of God came to "save his people from their sins" (Matt. 1:21); but it cost him his life.

Was the great sacrifice upon Calvary made only for a favored few? Hear the precious words from the Book of books: "For God so loved the world, that he gave his only begotten Son, that whosoever believeth in him should not perish, but have everlasting life. For God sent not his Son into the world to condemn the world; but that the world through him might be saved'' (John 3:16-17). The Son of man came to seek and to save that which was lost (Luke 19:10).

Oh, how sweet these words must sound to the one who is lost in sin, and has become awakened to the awful fact that the agonies of perdition are near at hand, unless a helping hand is stretched forth to deliver from the eternal burning!

It is a blessed thing to know that a way has been opened whereby people can be saved from all their iniquities, and have the stains and guilt of sin entirely removed, never more to be remembered against them. But so many fail to obtain this precious gift which has been offered free to all; surely there must be some secret or way of understanding it. There is something about it that confounds the wise of this world; the great minds of the age can not comprehend nor gainsay; infidels and skeptics fail to reason away, and unbelievers of every description with all their unbelief can not change it in the least; can not lessen its power or overthrow its doctrine, because it emanates from heaven, and was planned by an all-wise Creator. How foolish it is for weak mortals of earth to undertake to reason away and overthrow the works and plans of God!

Men have spent months and years, yea, even their whole life trying to overthrow and disprove the doctrine of salvation, and yet, before closing their eyes in death, had to acknowledge their error, and that salvation is a reality, and confess that their doom was sealed for eternity because of their unbelief. Many would-be skeptics, as death stared them in the face in the last hours of life, and the closing scenes brought to view a glimpse of eternity, would have gladly given wordly possessions and everything dear on earth for a few hours more of life, and a chance to meet the conditions required to obtain what had been rejected, despised, and opposed. But alas! Too late! They that sow to the wind must reap the whirlwind; and they who oppose the truth of God in this life until death overtakes them, must abide his wrath throughout eternity in the flames and torments of hell.

Many have tried to search out the deep things of God in their own strength, but have made a complete failure. Great masterly minds have spent years of reasoning trying with their chain of logic to unravel the mysteries of the word of God, or to harmonize it with some freak of nature. But we read that "the natural man receiveth not the things of the Spirit of God: for they are foolishness unto him: neither can he know them, because they are spiritually discerned." (1 Cor. 2:14).

It is no difficult matter then to see why people fail to understand God and his word, or the ways of his salvation. They do not learn the secret, therefore fail to find the way.

The Basis
Of Salvation

by
Charles E. Brown

Excerpted from *The Meaning of Salvation,* by Charles E. Brown (Anderson, Ind.: Gospel Trumpet Company, Copyright © 1944).

IF THERE is one doctrine upon which all historic Christianity is agreed it is the fundamental teaching that salvation is made available to mankind through the sacrifice of Jesus Christ. This sacrifice is usually taken to mean the whole history of Christ's incarnation, passion, death, and Resurrection, although frequently only one aspect of this divine drama is taken as representative of them all. That salvation is the result of the entire life and work of Christ is evident in the language of Paul, said of Christ Jesus: "Who, being in the form of God, thought it not robbery to be equal with God: but made himself of no reputation, and took upon him the form of a servant, and was made in the likeness of men: and being found in fashion as a man, he humbled himself, and became obedient unto death, even the death of the cross. Wherefore God also hath highly exalted him, and given him a name which is above every name: that at the name of Jesus every knee should bow, of things in heaven, and things in earth, and things under the earth; and that every tongue should confess that Jesus Christ is Lord, to the glory of God the Father'' (Phil. 2:6-11). This passage traces the redemption of mankind to the entire work of Christ in all his incarnation, suffering, death, Resurrection, and ascension to glory.

The most able minds of the church have pondered for generations upon the meaning of the atonement—what was it that made Christ's death necessary? The Scriptures teach that Christ's death was a ransom, but to whom? The ancient Greek fathers taught that Christ's death was a ransom to Satan. Satan had acquired a certain control over man and had brought him into bondage, and Christ was given by the Father as a ransom to Satan in order to buy the souls of men back to God. Gregory of Nyssa taught this theory in what was perhaps its crudest form, namely, that Christ was like the bait on a fishhook which Satan accepted, not being able to perceive the divinity of Christ hidden under the forms of his humiliation. Therefore Satan took hold of Christ, but he was not powerful enough to maintain Christ in his grasp. This theory has been regarded as impossible and absurd for perhaps a thousand years, but it has recently been revived in a modified form by Gustaf Aulen of the Theological School of Lund, Sweden. Aulen has professed to see in this old theory an approximation to the truth that man's state is self-contradictory, for although he has by a sad apostasy perverted himself into an abnormal condition under the devil's sway, he is nevertheless a creature of God who rightly belongs to God. Aulen thinks this old theory is an attempt to show that although the relationship between God and

Satan is hostile, God would not use force in accomplishing his purpose.

The theory that the death of Christ was a ransom to Satan held the field from the days of Origen, who died A.D. 254, until a new interpretation was made by Anselm, Archbishop of Canterbury, who died A.D. 1109. Anselm taught that sin is debt (guilt) and that under the government of God it is absolutely necessary that this debt shall be paid, or that the penalty incurred by the guilt of sin shall be suffered either by the sinner or by a satisfactory substitute. This doctrine has become the orthodox interpretation of the universal church. The Council of Trent wrote: "Jesus Christ who, when we were enemies, merited justification for us by his most sacred passion on the tree and satisfied God the Father for us"; so holds the Roman Catholic Church and this view is re-echoed by the Lutheran Formula of Concord, the Heidelberg Catechism, the second Helvetic Confession, the Westminister Confession, and the Thirty-nine Articles of the Church of England. There have been a number of minor theories unnecessary to specify here. The most prominent orthodox digression from the Anselmic interpretation is that called the governmental theory, propounded by Hugo Grotius, who died 1645. Grotius taught that the law is the product of the divine will and the right to relax its demands at will belongs to God's prerogative of moral governor, but since the free remission of the penalty in the case of some sinners would weaken the motives restraining from disobedience the subjects of the divine government in general by affording an example of impunity, the benevolence of God requires that as a precondition of the forgiveness of any sinners he should furnish such an example of suffering in Christ as would exhibit his determination that sin shall not escape with impunity. This is called the government theory because it emphasizes the fact that the sufferings of Christ were not an exact substitute for the sinner but were made a moral equivalent in the divine system of government.

This theory was carried over into the Arminian theology

and was taken up by the Wesleyan theologians with modifications, the purpose being to avoid the conclusion of the Calvinists that if Christ died for any man that man would be saved regardless of anything which he might do. Wesleyan theologians sought to get away from such a mechanical theory. This doctrine has been thinned out by liberals into something like the moral theory of atonement. On the other hand, it can be interpreted in an orthodox manner as by the great Dutch theologian, Philip Limborch, who wrote: "The death of Christ is called a sacrifice for sin, but sacrifices are not payment of debt, nor are they full satisfactions for sins. But a gratuitous remission is granted when they are offered."

We do not regard it necessary to arouse further controversy on the subject by proposing any ingenious interpretation of the atonement. It is enough to leave it where the New Testament placed it and say that in some way, possibly beyond human understanding in this life, "God so loved the world, that he gave his only begotten Son, that whosoever believeth in him should not perish, but have everlasting life."

The Problem
Of Depravity
by
Charles W. Naylor

Excerpted from *Winning a Crown,* by C. W. Naylor (Anderson, Ind.: Gospel Trumpet Company, 1919).

AMONG the practical effects of depravity in a regenerated person, is that he can not love God perfectly. There is a frequent assertion of the self-life. It is so easy for him to think that his way is right and best. And in spite of his desire to please and serve God, there is, nevertheless, within him a something that causes him to want his own way, to want to gratify his own personal desires. There is a twofoldness about his desires. There is a something that desires to please God, and at the same time another something that desires to please himself. This latter is sometimes very strong, and may occasion him no little difficulty when he endeavors to submit himself in the will of God. Through grace he may overcome this and submit to God, but he can not of himself destroy it. It is quite true that we can never become automatically unselfish; but it is also true that the strength of the self-life is depravity, and that, when this is destroyed, we can much more easily and more naturally be unselfish.

Temptation more forcefully takes hold of one when he is in the regenerate state than it does when he is in the wholly sanctified state, because under the former conditions it receives cooperation from depravity. A brother in telling of his personal experience spoke on this wise: "Temptations used to seem to get right up close to me and to take hold upon me. I used, oftentimes, to have a terrible battle with them; but now it seems that things are changed. Temptations do not get close to me as they did then. There seems to be a something that holds them off at a distance from me so that they do not have the power that they used to have; nor does it take the struggle to overcome them that it used to take."

This brother's experience has been duplicated by the experiences of the writer and thousands of others. There is something within the regenerated man that seems to answer to temptation; and he must resist, not only the temptation, but also that something within himself upon which the temptation takes hold. I refer, not simply to his natural propensities (for these natural propensities will persist in the sanctified state), but rather to the depraved state of these natural propensities. When we are in the regenerated

Characteristic Doctrinal Emphases

state, our natural desires are more inclined to run in unlawful channels and are harder to restrain than they are when we are in the wholly sanctified state. The more grace we have, the more our desires are restrained without apparent effort. Grace overwhelms many desires or tendencies in our natural being, making it the more possible for us to guide ourselves in the way of God with ease. The more grace we have, the more easily we can keep ourselves in perfect standing before God and the more perfectly conform to his will. The less of grace we have, the less of power we have to do this.

The warfare between grace and depravity in a regenerated person uses up spiritual strength, and consequently limits his activities in other directions. We can not accomplish things for God as we might, if we have to use so much of our strength upon ourselves, and so, for this reason the obtaining of release from depravity enables us more fully to throw our energies into the life of salvation and the work of God; the greater grace that we possess when sanctified, increases our spiritual powers and makes us very much more able to accomplish work for God than we otherwise could do. We can thus glorify him in a greater degree. Regenerated people are to a degree conscious of this inner conflict; but they can not be as conscious of the distinction between the two different states of grace as can the one who has entered the higher state. They must have the personal experience in order to know for themselves.

Two remedies for this depraved state have been proposed. The first is the repression remedy; that is, depravity must be kept in subjection through life by the will. Those teaching this theory hold that there can be no elimination of this element, no cleansing from it, but that it is of such a nature that it will ever be with us through the journey of life and that we must continually watch and guard against its asserting itself, lest it should overthrow us and lead us astray from God. According to this theory, life is a continued and unending warfare against it. Their only hope of ending this warfare is in death; they expect to be sanctified at death and not to take this element with them into heaven. Such as these are ready to exclaim with the apostle Paul, "Oh, wretched man that I am!" but they are not able to join with him in the song of deliverance.

The other remedy, that of eradication, is taught by people who believe in a second work of divine grace. The teaching of these, however, frequently runs into an idealism that leaves nothing whatever to repress in our natures. According to this extreme position, we should become practically automatons. Advocates of such teaching like to picture sanctification as making us a sort of angelic beings; and they would have us live in an ecstatic state, high above the practical affairs of life. They can tell us just how glorious we should feel on all occasions; how rapturous it is to dwell in that condition. Their teaching is idealism pure and simple.

The true idea, it seems to me, can not be expressed by the extreme teachings of either of these theories. As is usually the case, the middle ground between the two extremes is the most tenable. Our human nature is a creation of God, and as such, it is a necessary part of us; and God will never destroy it, in fact, he can not destroy it without destroying us. Sanctification, therefore, is not the destruction of this nature, but is the purification of it. It corrects the abnormal spiritual condition and brings the natural into a condition in which it may regain a proper balance. Paul said, "I keep under my body, and bring it into subjection" (1 Cor. 9:27). All the faculties and propensities of our nature are for our service and use. We are to master them. The will is to rule them and have them in subjection to itself and, as a result, to righteousness also.

Elements
Of True Bible Holiness
by
Herbert M. Riggle

Excerpted from the *Gospel Trumpet,* January 13, 1940.

HOLINESS is the heart of the church and of our religion. It is the vital element in our Christian experience and life.

During the World War, I held an evangelistic meeting in Saskatoon, Saskatchewan, Canada. Every day the trains on the Canadian Pacific Railroad were unloading wounded and maimed soldiers from the battlefields of France. On a certain day a young woman of the city was informed that her husband would arrive, and she, of course, went to the station to meet him. As she stood there in expectancy, two soldiers carried him off the train in a clothes basket. Both limbs were off close up to his body, and both arms were missing. He was just the stub of a man. The minute she saw him she went violently insane. From this incident I got a lesson that I shall never forget. That man could also have lost both eyes, his ears, his teeth, and other parts of his body, and still lived. He would, of course, have been far from normal, but he could have existed nevertheless. But there is one member of his body vital, and without it, he could not have lived a moment. That is his heart.

This is true with the church, individually and collectively. Paul, in 1 Corinthians 12, likens the church to the human body. Every part is essential to its proper functioning; but there is one element absolutely vital, and that is *holiness*. I repeat, it is the heart of our Christian experience and life. Without genuine holiness, your profession is vain, empty, worthless, and your religion is false and a sham. You may claim orthodoxy in your doctrine and teaching, and be as strict as a Pharisee in your practice, but without genuine Bible holiness your religion is useless. Wesley knew this, and stressed holiness beyond all else. It is essential to unity among God's people. A religious group may see eye to eye in teaching, be committed to the outward practice of all the rites and ordinances of the church, and yet be rent asunder by jealousy, envy, faultfinding, lack of confidence, and a hundred related elements. We often see this. Jesus prayed the Father to sanctify believers "that they may be one." Sanctification alone will produce this oneness.

True holiness will enable men and women to fill places of responsibility without exaltation and lordship on their part, and at the same time without envy and jealousy and evil surmising on the part of their brethren. It is essential to the successful prosecution and carrying forth of the tremendous task assigned to the ministry and church—world-evangelism.

Briefly, the constituent elements of Bible holiness may be summed up as follows: God himself is the originating cause. His infinite wisdom schemed the plan. His infinite love provided it, and now his infinite power effects it in our hearts and lives. He is the spring and fountain from which it flows. Thus we are "partakers of his holiness." Next, the blood of Christ is the procuring cause. "Wherefore Jesus also, that he might sanctify the people with his own blood, suffered without the gate" (Heb. 13:12). The Holy Ghost is the effecting efficient cause: "being sanctified by the Holy Ghost" (Rom. 15:16). The gospel is the instrumental cause: "Sanctify them through thy truth" (John 17:17). Faith is the conditional cause: "Sanctified by faith that is in me" (Acts 26:18).

In considering the results of genuine holiness I shall treat the matter both negatively and positively. It will not transform us into deities or angels. It will not destroy our natural appetites, passions, temperaments, and dispositions. However, it will enable us to govern and control these and keep them in proper place. It will not save us from temptations and severe trials; will not make us immune to sin, unless we constantly watch and pray, and daily receive a fresh supply of grace. It will not save from human weaknesses, but will enable us to overcome many of them.

On the positive side, perfected holiness in entire sanctification will completely destroy and cleanse out of our hearts every impure, unholy, and sinful temper and disposition. This list includes carnal anger, envy, jealousy, pride, lust, love of praise, touchiness, stubbornness, insubordination, sullenness, and dozens of related traits of the "old man of sin." The happy recipient of this second grace is made pure, even as He is pure. "As he is, so are we in this world" (1 John 4:17).

Perfection Leads
To Unity
by
Jacob W. Byers

Excerpted from *Sanctification,* by J. W. Byers (Moundsville, W.Va.: Gospel Trumpet Publishing Company, 1902).

CHRISTIAN PERFECTION is not maturity in wisdom, grace, or knowledge. "Ye therefore, beloved, seeing ye know these things before, beware lest ye also, being led away with the error of the wicked, fall from your own steadfastness. But grow in grace, and in the knowledge of our Lord and Savior Jesus Christ" (2 Pet. 3:17-18).

Christian perfection is looked upon by some as an impossibility in this life; but when we turn to the Word of God and see the many plain texts upon the subject, it must become evident to every candid mind that it is in the plan of redemption that every child of God should attain to it. It would not be according to the nature of divine grace to require of us anything we could not do. No reasonable earthly parent would demand an impossibility of a child, and it is certain that our heavenly Father would not command us to be "perfect even as he is perfect" unless he has provided abundant grace to bring us up to this blessed experience. According to our own power or ability we could never reach such an exalted plane, for it is not within the power of man to change his depraved nature, and every self-effort to reach a state of perfection is but vain. But God is able to make all grace abound and as an all-wise Father he has made it possible that we should be perfect.

From the scriptures quoted we can plainly see that the perfection required of us is reasonable and just. Had he commanded us to be perfect in knowledge, wisdom, judgment, or in anything else in an absolute sense, we would be forced to the conclusion that God has either required an impossibility of us or it is not for us to attain in this life and therefore belongs only to the resurrected state. But we can clearly see the nature of his requirements and that they are all within the limits of his grace toward us in this life.

Oh, that every child of God could see the imperative need of an absolute consecration and then cheerfully and voluntarily meet the conditions of the same, so that God could fill each heart with love, and cause each one to know what it means to love God with all our heart. As long as our affections are divided between God and anything else, our love is not perfect; and until the regenerate heart has made the scriptural consecration, there will be a divided condition of the affections. The obedient regenerate heart dwells in God, and thus is taught of God the necessity of the perfect consecration, which, when fully complied with, enables the perfect cleansing to become effected. The apostle John says, "Herein is our love made perfect," and "his love is perfected in us."

No one can ever be fully satisfied in this redemption life until this second work of grace is accomplished in the heart. Justification brings us into the blessed kingdom of God's love. Sanctification perfects his love in us. This second grace enables us to realize not only the meaning of perfect love, but we also comprehend the glorious fact that God has wrought in us perfect purity and holiness. This implies our being perfect in God's will, because we have yielded our will completely to him. Every disposition of our will which sought its own way is now in perfect conformity with his; and as Jesus could say in Gethsemane, "Thy will be done," which meant death on Calvary to him, so we have said the same to God with a vivid consciousness that once for all it meant death to us. It has required the perfect will of Jesus to obtain this grace of sanctification for us, and it now requires our perfect will to receive it from him. Here is where we can stand perfect and complete in all the will of God.

Another beautiful characteristic of sanctification is perfect unity. One of the most striking features of the religious world today is division among those who profess to believe in and follow Christ. There is no greater evil existing than this. Men have made creeds and sects and have persuaded the people to join them, until the disgusting spectacle of division is seen everywhere, and the non-professing world is amazed at the sickening sight. Hireling preachers are pleading for their respective denominations, and while many honest children of God are dissatisfied with this sad state of affairs, they are taught from the pulpit that God has made these divisions and it is the duty of every Christian to join and support them. But such is not the will of God; he has designed that his people should all be one, and in his prayer Jesus expresses the extent of this unity: "That they all may be one; as thou, Father, art in me, and I in thee, that they also may be one in us" (John 17:21). This certainly implies a wonderful and perfect unity. Many sect advocates cry, "Impossible, impossible; God's people can not be one." But the whole theme of Jesus' prayer is unity. As we carefully read this prayer we can readily perceive the divine method to effect this unity. It is plain and simple: "Sanctify them through thy truth: thy word is truth. . . . Neither pray I for these alone, but for them also which shall believe on me through their word; that they all may be one" (John 17:17, 20). Then in Heb. 2:11 we see again that this is God's plan—"For both he that sanctifieth and they who are sanctified are all of one."

A New Approach
To Sanctification
by
Charles E. Brown

Excerpted from the *Gospel Trumpet,* November 6, 1954.

I HAVE been preaching the doctrine of entire sanctification for nearly sixty years. I do not say this to create the impression that I know all about it, but to calm any fears that I might be putting forth some strange, heretical teaching on the subject I have loved and taught so long.

Let us come to our subject from a new viewpoint. It is the same palace shining bold and bright in the golden sunlight of truth, but we shall see another side of it.

Throughout all the years we have been approaching this palace for study from the standpoint of purity. That is a glorious side of the palace and not one word we have said is false. "Blessed are the pure in heart: for they shall see God" (Matt. 5:8). "Follow . . . holiness without which no man shall see the Lord" (Heb. 12:14).

At the same time there are many professed Christians who on account of false teaching regard all talk of purity of heart in Christians as simple, unmasked hypocrisy. We know they are dead wrong; they are against the Bible. But it is almost useless to assault their prejudice head on. Let us try another way.

There is an outstanding truth of the doctrine of holiness that we have neglected for a long time. It is this: The holy thing is the thing that belongs to God. For purposes of study, this is probably the best approach to the subject. At least, it is worth trying after such long neglect.

Before men knew much about being pure in heart, they knew a great deal about things belonging to God. This is the road of knowledge by which men came to learn about holiness. It is the kindergarten of religious instruction. In ancient times God took the human race upon his knee and began to teach them by the pictures of sacrifice in the red light of burning altar fires.

Now, in order to carry on the sacrificial system, it was necessary to have a large amount of equipment—altars, victims, sacrificial instruments such as knives and bowls and the like, and in the history of Israel a tent or temple, grounds, priests, and equipment of all kinds.

From the very beginning, this entire stock of material was reckoned as belonging to God—and it was that fact alone which made it esteemed as holy. The holy was always and only that which belonged to God. "Whatsoever toucheth the altar shall be holy" (Exod. 29:37). "The altar . . . sanctifieth the gift" (Matt. 23:19). And that was all because whatever was put on the altar at that moment began to belong to God and could not be retaken by the man making the sacrifice.

Holiness teachers have always known this, but in our haste to get on to the teaching of purity, we have pointed out that this phase of holiness is "ceremonial" holiness and as such only a type of the real thing.

Granted, the holiness of the redeemed is a deeper thing than the holiness of the altar of the ancient temple. Nevertheless, we must not hurry past this altar too fast, for it and its accompaniments were like the very alphabet itself without which we cannot spell out the meaning of the holy and of holiness.

The very first thing we can say about the holy man is that he belongs to God. And just as certainly we can say with the absolute assurance of stating a mathematical axiom: Every man who belongs to God is holy.

Some holiness fighters have taken an unholy delight in holding up to ridicule all believers in holiness as being shameless hypocrites professing to be holy, when they think that no man on earth can claim such sinless perfection. Let us not debate about what kind of man a holy man may or must be. Suffice it to say that we can prove to any educated, intelligent man that any and every man who belongs to God is holy.

Now, let us get this clear in our minds. Many things that we believe implicitly cannot be proved because of the nature of the facts and the limitations of logical proof. That is why we can prove mathematical statements easily but are not able to prove that democracy is the best form of government even when we believe it enough to die for our belief.

Just so, we can prove up to the hilt and beyond any contradiction that every man who belongs to God is holy, for that is the very definition of "holy" that theology started out with many years ago.

The next question would be: What kind of man would a holy man be? This question arose long after the definition of the holy as that which belongs to God. The answer was probably wrought out of the common reasoning regarding the loyalty of good slaves to their masters. A good slave would love his master and be loyal to him. In time he would come to see things as his master viewed them. He would grow into the likeness of his master. If his master was a good man, he would be a good man. If his master was kind, honest, and just, he would become kind, honest, and just.

Then, as throughout all the ages, the thought of religious people lifted from man to God. And revelation paved a path from man's parable to God's eternal truth. God's man must be like God. To be holy is to belong to God; to belong to God is to be morally like God. Hence, to be holy is to be good, like God.

Hitherto, in our haste to establish the doctrine with shorthand logic, we have leaped this gap. It was always there: we just hurried past it. Let us go back and clear up this point.

Let us not insist too much upon how good we are (not denying it), but let us emphasize this truth that we have only the minimum standard for any Christian: We belong to God. No Christian can fall short of that. No person who is such can fail to be holy. Let us turn the tables for a little while and show our Christian friends that we claim not one whit more than they do. All Christians are holy.

In religion the term for holy people who belong to God is "saints." And any theologian in Protestantism will tell you that every holy person is a saint, and every saint is holy.

What about sanctification as a second-crisis experience? The very fact that the primary meaning of holy is "belonging to God" does help clear up the difference between sanctification (in conversion) and entire sanctification (in the second crisis). Every man who has ever had any dealings in real estate knows that there are, regardless of common opinion, all kinds of problems and puzzles in the question of ownership of real estate or of any property.

Before making a few hints at a solution, let us remember that the question of our real relation to God is an ineffable mystery revealed to us by these parables, such as sonship, ownership, debtor's relation, and even marriage to Christ through our membership in the church, his bride. The new birth can be only a metaphor, a short parable; we have to be satisfied with figures of speech until the light eternal banishes the shadows of our finite ignorance.

In such figures of speech we see a justified man as a house which was stolen from its rightful owner by legal chicanery, now in the court of God. Christ wins the clear title to our souls (that house), but not yet is all the enemy's furniture removed. Not yet has the Master taken full possession (wholly sanctified) of that which is legally his.

I am well aware of the inadequacy of all this. But space is limited. The Bible teaches a second crisis so plainly that we feel ourselves obliged to trace out so far as possible some few of the insights which go to show how reasonable and simple that truth really is.

But remember this: You do not have to know the chemical analysis of honey in order to eat it. All you need to know is where it is and how to get it. When you get it, it will justify and explain itself. All explanation is futile except that which opens the road to the honey. That is what I have sought to do here.

Baptism
Of the Holy Spirit
by
Boyce W. Blackwelder

Excerpted from the *Gospel Trumpet,* May 19, 1956.

THE WORK of the Holy Spirit embraces the whole of the Christian life, every aspect and development of the believer's experience being included in his activity. While the Spirit is present in the converted heart, he takes possession in a greater way in the Pentecostal enduement of power. To the disciples before Pentecost, Jesus said of the Holy Spirit's presence, ''Ye know him; for he dwelleth with you, and shall be in you'' (John 14:17).

In the redemption of an individual there is a difference between the birth of the Spirit and the baptism of the Spirit. That is to say, there is an operation of the Holy Spirit which is distinct from and supplementary to his regenerating work.

The two definite works of the Holy Spirit in human redemption are necessary because of the nature of sin. According to the Scriptures, sin exists in two basic forms: committed and inherited; or willful transgression and a perverted moral nature.

Thus a distinction is made between sin and sins, between sin as root and sin as fruit, between sin as state and sin as act. Because of these two types of sin man has a twofold need. First he needs forgiveness for committed sin. And, second, he needs to be made pure in heart.

Conversion meets the first need. It deals with man's willful sins, the believer being justified before God (Rom. 5:1) and regenerated in his own heart (2 Cor. 5:17), these being the objective and subjective aspects of the new birth (John 3:7).

But a deeper experience is required to deal with the principle of sin, the innate tendency or proclivity toward evil. The general belief of Christians is that inbred sin or depravity in some sense remains in the believer after regeneration.

Does not every converted person soon become aware of an intense spiritual struggle? Is there not within him the vestige of original sin, a foreign element not yet expelled, a usurper, an actual ally of Satan, a traitor in the camp, always ready to open the soul's door to the enemy? Is not the regenerate man still a needy man?

God's redemptive grace meets the utmost human need. John foretold the method of divine deliverance from the contamination of sin when he contrasted water baptism with the fiery baptism of the Holy Spirit (Matt. 3:11-12). Water baptism symbolizes the regenerating work of the Spirit. Fire is the emblem of the purifying effected when the Spirit is received in his fullness.

Bible students agree than on Pentecost the disciples of Jesus received an extraordinary spiritual experience. One of two theological positions must be taken: Either the disciples were not converted until Pentecost, or, having been converted previously, they received at Pentecost a deeper work of grace—the baptism of the Holy Spirit.

It is clear from the New Testament context (Matt. 10:1; Luke 10:17-20; John 14:17; 17:9, 12, 16) that the disciples were converted before Pentecost. That is to say, prior to Pentecost they were born of the Spirit. At Pentecost they were baptized with the Spirit, an instantaneous experience whereby their hearts were purified (Acts 2:1-4; 15:9).

The New Testament records other occasions when believers received the baptism or infilling of the Holy Spirit. The Samaritans after becoming baptized believers in Christ through the preaching of Philip, received a deeper work of the Spirit under the ministry of Peter and John (Acts 8:12-17).

Paul, after his conversion on the Damascus Road, was filled with the Holy Spirit during the visit of Ananias, who came for that purpose (9:17). After the twelve disciples at Ephesus had participated in baptism characterized by repentance, Paul instructed them more fully, and they received the deeper work of the Holy Spirit (19:1-7).

That the baptism of the Holy Spirit received at Pentecost was a representative experience—the norm or standard for the gospel dispensation—is indicated by Peter's words: "The promise is unto you, and to your children, and to all that are afar off, even as many as the Lord our God shall call" (Acts 2:39).

Therefore, we conclude that the baptism of the Holy Spirit is God's plan for believers, that it is an experience to be received after conversion, and that it is the means by which the believer's heart is cleansed from all sin. Thus the believer is brought into full salvation, the privilege of Christians under the gospel.

Holiness (sanctification) begins in conversion and reaches its culmination in the baptism of the Holy Spirit. The Apostle Paul prayed for justified persons that God might sanctify them wholly (1 Thess. 5:23). By divine inspiration, Paul adds to his petition the words of assurance: "Faithful is he that calleth you, who also will do it" (v. 24). Entire sanctification is a New Testament doctrine.

The baptism of the Holy Spirit involves both crisis and growth. Grace is not static but is always dynamic. Crises in spiritual experience characterize beginnings, not terminations. No doubt many Christians have failed to make spiritual progress because they have been content with obtainment and have not realized the importance of attainment. In the highest Christian life growth and development continue in the grace that is received instantaneously.

On occasions after their Pentecostal baptism, the disciples are said to have been filled with the Holy Spirit (Acts 4:8, 31). These incidents indicate that in addition to their original baptism or infilling, believers may receive special anointings of the Spirit from time to time, and that the normal, Spirit-filled life is one which is constantly motivated by the Holy Spirit.

After the crisis work of the Holy Spirit by which the believer is made pure in heart and endued with power for service, progress is necessary to achieve one's maximum potential in Christian fruitfulness.

We should remember that in this glorious experience man has a part to do as well as God; that there are both the gift and the task, both realization and aspiration. The Christian experience is a matter of a moment and a matter for a lifetime.

Spiritual Gifts
For the Church

by
Albert F. Gray

Excerpted from *Christian Theology*, by Albert F. Gray (Anderson, Ind.: Warner Press, Copyright © 1946).

A Time to Remember: TEACHINGS

THE PROMISE of Christ, "You shall receive power when the Holy Spirit has come upon you" (Acts 1:8), finds a part of its fulfillment in the spiritual gifts that are given to God's children. Every child of God receives power for testimony. The manifestations of the Spirit through spiritual gifts greatly strengthen that testimony.

1. **The Nature of Spiritual Gifts**—Our information concerning spiritual gifts must be found in the New Testament. The most extended discussion is found in 1 Corinthians 12 to 14. Elsewhere gifts are mentioned also and evidences of their use are found in several places.

(1) *Gifts distinguished from graces.* The graces, or fruits of the Spirit, are to be distinguished from spiritual gifts. This is not to say that they are to be segregated in actual practice or that a person can be filled with one and have none of the other. They are closely related; for instance, the gift of faith works by the grace of love. But for the sake of analysis they are considered separately. A list of the fruits of the Spirit is found in Galations 5.

(2) *They are not natural abilities.* Many people are gifted with unusual abilities. When these are consecrated to God the Spirit will use them to his glory. They are of great value in the work of the Lord. However, these abilities are a part of one's personality and can be used for self as well as for God. They differ from spiritual gifts in that they are a natural inheritance, or development.

(3) *They are supernatural enduements of power.* Spiritual gifts are supernatural powers bestowed by the Spirit upon individuals to be exercised for the glory of God in the interests of the whole church. They are special qualifications for service. Although these gifts are under the rational control of the possessor, he cannot exercise them wholly at his own will, but only in cooperation with the Spirit.

2. **A List of Gifts.**—A list of nine gifts is given in 1 Corinthians 12 and a few others are named in Romans 12. It is not claimed that these lists include all the actual or possible

gifts of the Spirit. Only a few of the gifts will be considered here.

(1) *The gift of prophecy.* The gift of prophecy, though it may make one eloquent, is not to be confused with natural eloquence and certainly not with elocution. The prophet is God's spokesman. The gift of prophecy makes one a prophet. It is that spiritual endowment which brings one into close union with the mind of God, enabling him to understand spiritual things and giving him power to proclaim them. One may speak well on various themes without the gift of prophecy. Likewise, he may have keen insight in social and political problems. But the Holy Spirit operating through the gift of prophecy enables the prophet to see spiritual things in their true light.

(2) *The gift of discernment.* The gift of discernment enables the possessor to discern spiritual things. He has a special insight into the operation of spiritual forces and is keen to detect evil spirits. A humble exercise of this gift is a protection to the church, but it must be distinguished clearly from suspicion, which is the cause of much trouble. Not all who imagine they were set in the body as an "eye" have the gift of discernment. This is a rather rare gift and is exercised only by the humble.

(3) *Miracles and healing.* Though God hears the prayers of all his children, there are some who possess the gift of miracles or of healing. Such persons are used in a remarkable way, particularly in the healing of the sick. Miracles can be wrought only by the Spirit, and the gift of miracles cannot be used at will by the possessor. This gift is such an evident manifestation of divine power that it is clearly distinguished from any mere mental power.

(4) *The gift of tongues.* This gift is declared to be the least valuable of all. It is the power given by the Spirit to speak in a language not previously known. It has no practical value except as a sign to unbelievers. So far as we have record, it was never used in preaching. The gift of tongues is not to be confused with the meaningless, hysterical utterances that are sometimes substituted for it.

3. **The Receiving of Gifts.**—It is clear from the record that spiritual gifts are received in connection with the baptism with the Spirit. Such was the case on the Day of Pentecost and on other occasions. However, it appears that gifts may be received at other times also. They are distributed as the Spirit wills, and hence are not to be sought for at the wish of the individual. It is not to be expected that any one person will possess all the gifts and neither is there any one gift possessed by everyone. The assumption that the gift of tongues is given to all as the evidence of the baptism with the Holy Spirit is without foundation and is contrary to Paul's express statement that not all have the gift of tongues.

4. **Permanency of the Gifts.**—It is the opinion of some people that the gifts of the Spirit were placed in the church for the first generation only and that they are no longer needed. The words of Paul are quoted: "Whether there be prophecies, they shall be done away; whether there be tongues, they shall cease; whether there be knowledge, it shall be done away" (1 Cor. 13:8, ASV). It is assumed these (except knowledge!) have been done away, while love remains. Since it does not appear that "that which is perfect" has come yet, it would seem gifts may be remaining also.

However, we must recognize the right of the Spirit to give gifts as he pleases, and it may be he does not give every gift in every congregation in every age. A conclusive proof that gifts have not ceased is that they are now found in the church. If some of the gifts, such as tongues, are seldom manifested this is because the Spirit does not see fit to bestow them. We must recognize in the Spirit the right of freedom of action. He may give such gifts as he wishes, withholding, if he will, some gifts mentioned in the Bible and possibly giving some not mentioned therein. It is for us to accept what he gives and to use them for God's glory and the profiting of the church.

What Is The Kingdom of God?

by
Kenneth E. Jones

Excerpted from *Seek First the Kingdom,* by Kenneth E. Jones (Anderson, Ind.: Warner Press, n.d.).

THE KINGDOM of God is the moral and spiritual power of Christ in his work as Messiah and Mediator between God and man. The rule of God is made manifest through Jesus Christ. All those who are submitted to his rule are the subjects of the Kingdom. Christ sits on the throne of each heart that is committed to God's will and rule.

The fact that Jesus is king—in the strictest sense only—of those who have consciously yielded themselves to His rule, is only a part of the whole truth. Jesus Christ is omnipotent God. "He is the visible expression of the invisible God, ruling head of all creation, because in him were created all things in heaven or on earth, visible and invisible, whether thrones or ruling powers, or rulers, or authorities; everything was created by him and for him" (Col. 1:15-16, author's translation).

Jesus, then, is king of all creation. Everything that is was made by him and for his own purposes. He rules over all creation in his providential wisdom. He made the sun and the stars, set them in their appointed places, and established the orbits of all their satellites. He spoke the plants and animals into existence and ordered their interrelationships, at which scientists marvel. He made man and put him in the world for his own divine purposes. And he rules over all these things according to his own will.

Christ rules, too, over the kingdoms and governments of men. He is the Lord of history, as well as the Lord of creation. Upon his head are many crowns. He has demonstrated his power over the destinies of nations since the creation of man, and will end all history in his own good time by the final judgment of every person who has ever lived.

Yet something more specific than this general lordship is meant by the Biblical concept of the kingdom of God. As revealed in the New Testament, the kingdom of God is the rule of Jesus the King in the hearts of all those who submit to the conditions for salvation and who then submit wholeheartedly to his rule.

First of all, we need to understand that the kingdom of God is spiritual and not physical. That is, it differs radically from all the kingdoms of this world by not having a human king sitting on a great throne-seat. Instead, Jesus sits on his throne in the life of each individual person who lives for him. He does not rule over a particular nationality, but over those who have been born again, and are therefore "of the spirit" (John 3:6; Rom. 8:4-6).

By saying that the kingdom of God is spiritual, we mean among other things that God, who is spirit (John 4:24), guides us and rules our lives through working in and with our spirits. A human king could only try to control the actions of our physical bodies but could not control our minds and our spirits even if he tried. Yet that is just what Jesus does. Instead of being concerned primarily with our bodies, he controls our bodies through our minds and hearts. The spiritual power through which he does this is what makes us call the Kingdom "spiritual."

Another reason we call the Kingdom a spiritual kingdom is that it is governed through the agency of the Holy Spirit—the Spirit of God. Jesus came preaching and healing in the power of the Spirit. He promised the church through the disciples that he would send the Holy Spirit into our hearts to serve as our personal Comforter, Companion, Counselor, Co-witness, Convictor, and Conductor (John

14:16, 26; 15:26; 16:7). The Holy Spirit is to be our Helper in all the ways in which we need help. He sets the members in the Kingdom in the way which pleases him (1 Cor. 12:18), and fills them with love so that they will work with God and with one another. So the spiritual kingdom of God is that realm in which the Holy Spirit dominates.

One of the hardest lessons for the disciples and the early church to learn was that the gospel was for the whole world and that the kingdom of God must therefore include people of all races and nationalities. The Jewish people had for so long thought of themselves as the only ones worthy of being called the people of God, that it was very hard for them to see anything else.

Yet, Jesus died for the sin of the whole world (Rom. 5:18). The death of Jesus purchased redemption for all men alike, whether Jew or Gentile, so that in God's sight our human descent makes no difference at all (Galatians 3:26-29; Ephesians 2:11-19). This means that all men, regardless of race or nationality, are given an equal opportunity to be a part of the kingdom of God.

The kingdom of God is established, not by human might, not even by the might of atomic bombs, but by the power of God. Since God himself establishes the Kingdom, it cannot be overthrown, but will be everlasting. Daniel had said (2:44): "And in the days of these kings shall the God of heaven set up a kingdom, which shall never be destroyed: . . . it shall stand for ever." In Isaiah 9:7, a passage previously cited, God promised "to establish it with judgment and with justice from henceforth even for ever." Peter called it an "everlasting kingdom" (2 Pet. 1:11).

The kingdom of God is eternal because it is set up by the might and power of the everlasting God himself, and not by the temporal power and authority of any human beings. When Jesus came announcing his kingdom, he performed miracles as signs that God was at work in the world. When John the Baptizer sent to ask if He were really the one who had been promised by God or not, Jesus answered by sending back word that he was fulfilling the prophecies of the

Old Testament by the miracles he was performing. By God's eternal power he established an eternal kingdom in this world.

The kingdom of God is now in existence in this present world. Jesus, as eternal King, rules over all Christians (Matt. 28:18; Eph. 1:20-22; 1 Pet. 3:22). One of the clearest statements by Jesus of the fact that he did set up the kingdom is Luke 16:16: "The law and the prophets were until John: since that time the kingdom of God is preached, and every man presseth into it." That is, the preaching of John the Baptizer marked the transition from the prophecies of the Old Testament and the fulfillment of the New Testament. Jesus said that the kingdom of God was then in the reach of those who were willing to press their way into it. The kingdom of God is now in existence. Jesus is reigning in the hearts of the redeemed. We need not look for any future fulfillment of the kingdom prophecies of the Old Testament.

The Nature
Of Christ's Kingdom

by
Herbert M. Riggle

Excerpted from *Christ's Kingdom and Reign,* by H. M. Riggle (Anderson, Ind.: Gospel Trumpet Company, 1918).

THE IDEA that the Messiah would establish a literal kingdom upon the earth originated with the Jews. Many of them placed literal interpretations upon those prophecies which foretold the coming of Christ, and as a result they expected him to set up a temporal throne, subdue the nations, and restore again the kingdom of Israel. This gross error led them to reject Christ, oppose his spiritual kingdom, and consent to his death. They wanted only an earthly kingdom, and hence rejected and crucified the Son of God. He did not meet their expectation, therefore he became a stumbling-block to them. He said, ''Ye do err, not knowing the scriptures'' (Matt. 22:29); ''My kingdom is not of this world: if my kingdom were of this world, then would my servants fight'' (John 18:36).

Jesus acknowledged himself a king, saying, ''To this end was I born, and for this cause came I into the world'' (v. 37); that is, to set up a kingdom and reign as a king. But he clearly sets forth the nature of his kingdom when he declared it to be not temporal or literal, but purely spiritual—''not of this world.'' Through all his teaching he endeavored to show the people that his mission was to establish the kingdom of heaven in the hearts of men and there reign as King of peace. ''And when he was demanded of the Pharisees, when the kingdom of God should come, he answered them and said, The kingdom of God cometh not with observation. Neither shall they say, Lo here! or, lo there! for, behold, the kingdom of God is within you'' (Luke 17:20-21). This positive text stands in square contradiction to the teaching of the modern advocates of a future literal reign upon earth.

The Pharisees evidently believed that Messiah would establish a temporal kingdom and set up his throne in Jerusalem. So as Christ claimed to be the true Messiah, they naturally asked him when the kingdom of heaven should come. How clear his answer: ''The kingdom of God cometh not with observation.'' This would not be true were it a literal kingdom, for such would come with observation. The fact that it ''cometh not with observation,'' or outward show, positively proves it to be a spiritual kingdom; Christ ruling and reigning in the hearts of his people. Yes, dear reader, ''it is your Father's good pleasure to give you the kingdom'' (Luke 12:32), even ''the kingdom of heaven,'' a kingdom greater than Alexander or Napoleon ever swayed scepter over. And all this you will find in the full salvation of Jesus Christ.

The vain, worldly expectation that the Messiah would establish a literal kingdom caused the Jews to reject him and his spiritual kingdom. They wanted only an earthly kingdom; hence rejected and crucified the Son of God. As soon as the church began to apostatize and to lose the glory of the spiritual kingdom, vain ambitions awakened the old Jewish desire for a literal kingdom. And so it has come to pass that at this time of dead formality we have a multitude of men teaching the same error and false hope that crucified Christ nearly nineteen hundred years ago; namely, a literal kingdom of Christ.

The Reign of Christ

by
Charles E. Brown

Excerpted from *The Reign of Christ,* by Charles E. Brown (Anderson, Ind.: Gospel Trumpet Company, Copyright © 1950).

EVERY competent Bible student knows that the main controversy between the New Testament preachers of Christ and the Jewish opposers was concerning the nature of the Kingdom. Very solemnly and very stubbornly the Jewish teachers of Christ's time rejected him and his message because the Kingdom and the King manifested in their time were not in conformity with their preconceived and prejudiced interpretation of the ancient prophecies.

Premillennialists hold that John the Baptist began the work of presenting a carnal, earthly kingdom to the Jews;

that Christ continued this offer for a time, and that Christ's plans were balked because the Jews rejected this kingdom. The facts are exactly opposite to that theory, for we notice that John the Baptist preached atonement and redemption and the forgiveness of sins in the very beginning of his ministry. "Behold the Lamb of God, which taketh away the sin of the world" (John 1:29), he taught. This was his way of presenting the Kingdom. "Repent ye: for the kingdom of heaven is at hand. . . . Prepare ye the way of the Lord, make his paths straight" (Matt. 3:2-3).

In other words, repentance and salvation were the beginning of the Kingdom in the doctrine of John. Salvation, not carnal, earthly rule, was the meaning of the Kingdom at the very beginning. Zacharias, the father of John the Baptist, predicted that in the remembrance of his holy covenant God "would grant unto us, that we being delivered out of the hand of our enemies might serve him without fear, in holiness and righteousness before him, all the days of our life"(Luke 1:74-75).John was "to give knowledge of salvation unto his people by the remission of their sins" (v. 77).

The Apostle Matthew tells us that the angel addressed Joseph as the son of David and commanded that the child who was to be born of Mary should be called Jesus (Joshua), for "he shall save his people from their sins" (1:21). Here the heir of David's house is to begin his rule *by saving mankind from sin.*

Almost everywhere in the Gospels the kingdom of God is represented as salvation from sin. And according to Paul, "flesh and blood cannot inherit the kingdom of God" (1 Cor. 15:50). This Kingdom is mentioned 139 times in the New Testament. And 118 of these instances are not mentioned by Scofield in his supposedly exhaustive treatment of the subject.

The Apostles understood that entering the kingdom of God was the same as salvation from sin, for when Christ likened *entering the kingdom* to a camel going through the eye of a needle, the disciples said, "Who then can be saved?" (Matt. 19:23-25). Jesus agreed with them that entering the Kingdom and *being saved* are the same thing, for he continued: "With men this is impossible; but with God all things are possible" (v. 26). Christ certainly did not consider the Kingdom offer withdrawn on the day of his triumphal entry, for even after his death and resurrection he spent the intervening forty days before his ascension "speaking of the things pertaining to the kingdom of God" (Acts 1:3).

Our king is our Savior: "I will be thy king: where is any other that may save thee" (Hos. 13:10).

The carnal kingdom of Israel, which the premillennialists expect to be set up in the future to rule all mankind, was at first set up in violation of God's will. It was never anything but God's second best as a carnal, earthly institution. And here is the proof: The Israelites went to Samuel and said: "Now make us a king to judge us like all the nations. But the thing displeased Samuel, when they said, Give us a king to judge us. And Samuel prayed unto the Lord. And the Lord said unto Samuel, Hearken unto the voice of the people in all that they say unto thee: for they have not rejected thee, but they have rejected me, that I should not reign over them. According to all the works which they have done since the day that I brought them up out of Egypt even unto this day, wherewith *they have forsaken me,* and served other gods, so do they also unto thee. Now therefore hearken unto their voice: howbeit yet protest solemnly unto them, and show them the manner of the king that shall reign over them" (1 Sam. 8:5-9).

It was always God's highest will that God himself should be king over Israel, and when at last the earthly kings of Israel failed from their thrones in Jerusalem, God himself restored the kingdom in its spiritual sense by placing it in the hands of the Lord Jesus Christ, David's greatest son.

Therefore, throughout the whole Bible the throne of David is not a symbol of Jewish, carnal rule, but the symbol of the rule of Christ in his saving and sanctifying power. On the Day of Pentecost, in the very highest tide of the Holy Spirit's power, Peter preached: "Men and brethren, let me freely speak unto you of the patriarch David. . . . Being a prophet, and knowing that God had sworn with an oath to him, that of the fruit of his loins, according to the flesh, he would raise up Christ to sit on his [David's] throne; he seeing this before spake of the resurrection of Christ. . . . This Jesus hath God raised up, whereof we all are witnesses. Therefore being by the right hand of God exalted, and having received of the Father the promise of the Holy Ghost, he hath shed forth this. . . . Therefore let all the house of Israel know assuredly, that God hath made that same Jesus, whom ye have crucified, both Lord and Christ'' (Acts 2:29-36).

Here the meaning is clear for all who will see it without prejudice. The promise of a son of David *to sit on David's throne* referred to the *resurrection of Christ;* his exaltation to heaven to sit on the right hand of God is a fulfillment of the prophecy. And the shedding forth of the Holy Spirit upon believers is a manifest proof that Christ *was reigning on David's throne* in Pentecostal times and will so continue to the end of all time. The conclusion which the Apostle draws is that all the Jews should now understand that the crucified Jesus has been made both Lord and Christ, that is, Messiah and King; for the word Lord (*kurios*) was applied as a title to the emperors of that time. The first act of Christ as King on the throne of David, which means the throne of God in heaven, was to send forth the baptism of the Holy Spirit on the Day of Pentecost.

Our Position
On the Church Question
by
Frederick G. Smith

Excerpted from *Yearbook of the Church of God: 1925,* ed. by Elver F. Adcock (Anderson, Ind.: Gospel Trumpet Company, 1925).

THE MOST distinctive doctrine held by us is what we understand to be the true scriptural teaching concerning the church. According to the Scripture standard, we emphasize the doctrine of Christian unity and insist that true unity is to be found, not through hierarchies and apostolical successions and priestly corporations and church synods and ecclesiastical organizations and human creeds, but in the Christ alone, by spiritual attachment to and moral correspondence with him. We hold sectarianism to be antiscriptural, and claim that sectarianism has resulted from two things in particular: the teaching and practice of unscriptural doctrines, and the substitution of the human for the divine in schemes of church organization and government. We regard every effort to organize the church of Christ humanly as being denominational and sectarian.

The reason for this particular view of the church may be set forth as follows: The Word of the Lord and the Spirit of the Lord constituted the divine elements in the primitive church. These characteristics differentiated it from all other social units and made it the church of God. The Word of the Lord was divinely revealed, and it was faithfully preached as the standard of faith. The Spirit of God, given to the church, united the hearts of individual believers to Christ, its ever-living Head, thus making possible the vital union of all the saved in one body through him. And more than this, the place that each member had in the Christian community was by virtue of a *charism*. The Holy Spirit bestowed upon its members powers and capacities necessary for the edification and work of the church, and, according to Paul, the *charismata* formed the basis of the offices in the church. There was no ecclesiastical office without a *charism*; but not all *charismata* were applicable to an office. Those which corresponded to permanent and invariable needs in the church formed the basis of offices, while the others did not.

The church of God movement contends that these two fundamental principles of the primitive church were largely lost during the period of apostasy following the introduction of Christianity. During the reign of Rome, the Word of God was supplanted by the doctrines, commandments, and traditions of men. And in place of that original concept of the church as made up of all spiritually regenerated believers whose only bond of union was their spiritual attachment to Christ through the Holy Ghost, the concept of the church which came to prevail was that of a humanly organized society patterned after the kingdoms of this world. Hence in place of the charismata as the basis of spiritual organization and government, there developed an ecclesiastical corporation whose authority was altogether positional in character, patterned afer the civil government of Rome.

What Is the Church?

by
W. Dale Oldham

Reprinted from the *Gospel Trumpet,* May 10, 1947.

A Time to Remember: TEACHINGS

WHAT is the true New Testament church? Let us begin our discussion by saying what the church is not. First, it is not a denomination—nor is it all denominations put together. It is not the group of people who come to your place or mine to Sunday school and have their names and addresses on the Sunday school class records. Neither is it a mere movement—not even a holiness movement. Nor is it composed of everything which calls itself the church. Its membership is not necessarily reflected in statistics published in the yearbook of some church or group of churches, and its ministers are not necessarily only ministers listed in such yearbooks. The church is not composed of everyone who believes just as I believe. Neither is it composed only of folk who have bowed at a public altar in some church.

Webster defines the church as being "the whole body of Christians." The word "Christian" itself means Christlike men and women. It is composed only of men and women who have been born again through a forgiving, regenerating, life-giving contact with the Lord Jesus Christ. In Ephesians 1, Paul calls the church "the body of Christ." In Romans 12:5 he writes, "So we, being many, are one body in Christ, and every one members one of another." The members spoken of are not denominations, but individual men and women. The one body spoken of is a corporate, not divided, unit in which all converted men and women are assimilated in a spiritual unity.

There is as definite a spiritual relationship between members of the New Testament church as there is between members of a family. John said, "If we walk in the light as he is in the light, we have fellowship one with another" (1 John 1:7). There is a spiritual fellowship among all twice-born children of God. If that fellowship is lacking, it is proof of a spiritual inadequacy in someone's personal religious experience. Christian unity is the product of Christian experience. Paul writes in 1 Corinthians 12 that there should be no schism—meaning division—in the body, but that the members should have the same care one for another. And later in the chapter he writes, "But now are they many members, yet but one body. And the eye cannot say unto the hand, I have no need of thee: nor again the head to the feet, I have no need of you" (vv. 20-21). In the thirteenth verse we read, "For by one spirit are we all baptized into one body, whether we be Jews or Gentiles, whether we be bond or free."

If Paul's concept of the church represents the true picture, then the New Testament church contains in its membership all saved people. Do not, however, confuse the congregation with the true church. For in the congregation are many of the unredeemed, the unconverted, who make no profession of godliness. The church, the true church, is composed only of the redeemed.

So the New Testament church is not a denomination in any sense of the word. Denominations are the product of personal differences and individual leadership. Jesus built the New Testament church. "I will build my church" (Matt. 16:18) said he nineteen centuries ago. In Ephesians 2:20 we read that the church was built on the "foundation of the apostles and prophets, Jesus Christ himself being the chief cornerstone." Peter did not build the church, nor did Paul, nor Wesley, Luther, or D. S. Warner. Christ built the church. Paul said, "I planted, Apollos watered; God gave the increase" (1 Cor. 3:6).

How do you become a member of the New Testament church? If you stay with the Word itself, you will see there is only one way by which a man can become a member of the church. That is by being born into it. This birth of which I speak is not a physical birth but a spiritual birth. It is that which Jesus had in mind when he said to Nicodemus, "Ye must be born again" (John 3:7).

In Acts 2:47 we read, "And the Lord added to the church daily such as should be saved." In Psalms 87:5 this interesting statement is made, "And of Zion it shall be said, This and that man was born in her." Christ is the only door of entrance into the church. In John 10:9 He is quoted as saying, "I am the door: by me if any man enter in, he shall be saved."

A Time to Remember: TEACHINGS

New Testament church membership, then, is based upon Christian experience, rather than upon mere acceptance by a certain group. A man may, by acceding to the demands of various fraternal groups, become a member of them— any number of them—but to become a member of the New Testament church one must repent of his sins, confess them, forsake them, and receive pardon from God through faith in Jesus Christ. This formula is not creedalism. It is New Testament doctrine, plainly stated time after time by Jesus and those who recorded his words and his will.

Neither is the name of this holy family of God left to choice. The Apostle Paul had nothing sectarian in mind when he spoke of the New Testament church as the church of God. His first letter to the Corinthian church was addressed: "Unto the church of God which is at Corinth, to them that are sanctified in Christ Jesus, called to be saints, with all that in every place call upon the name of Jesus Christ our Lord, both theirs and ours." Time after time Paul speaks of the church of God. In Romans 16:16 he writes, "The churches of Christ salute you." We are told that the whole family both in heaven and in earth is named after the father of our Lord Jesus Christ, who is God. So it is the family of God, or the church of God.

Never should this name be applied in any sectarian sense. Never should it designate merely one small, separate, partisan group of God's people. The name "the church of God" is all-inclusive, so far as redeemed men and women are concerned. Every converted man, woman, and child is in the church of God. The ungodly, the unregenerate, those who have never experienced the new birth, are not in the church of God, regardless of what their religious affiliation may be. The New Testament church contains in its membership all the converted and none but the converted. Thus it is not only an all-inclusive church, but also an exclusive church.

The discipline of the New Testament church is the New Testament itself, which is spoken of as the perfect law of liberty. In 2 Timothy 3:16-17, Paul writes, "All scripture is

148 (388)

given by inspiration of God, and is profitable for doctrine, for reproof, for correction, for instruction in righteousness, that the man of God may be perfect, throughly furnished unto all good works." Thus the New Testament furnishes an adequate discipline for the church. In John 1:17 we read, "Law was given by Moses, but grace and truth came by Jesus Christ." The New Testament tells what the qualifications of a true minister should be. It tells what kind of character he must have. It tells how ministers should conduct the ordinances of God's house. It gives instruction as to their ordination, tells them how to deal with the sick, with erring members, with habitual trouble makers, provides principles by which all life is to be guided and governed. Members of the church are informed as to what are their duties toward each other and how to proceed in case of trespass.

Christianity has changed so radically in some respects through the centuries that it is sometimes refreshing to forget what one sees from day to day in the guise of the church and read instead what the New Testament has to say about it. Churches come and churches go, but the New Testament church goes on forever. Jesus said of it, "The gates of hell shall not prevail against it" (Matt. 16:18). Let our first loyalty be to the Lord Jesus Christ and to the church which is his body and which owns him alone as Lord. Let all else be secondary. Let dividing lines between true Christians be ignored or broken down. Let there be full fellowship among all of God's people.

Jesus prayed that we might all be one. Another wrote that we ought to endeavor to keep the unity of the spirit in the bonds of peace. Geographical or social division lines need not hinder the full fellowship of all the people of God. Let us do all within our power to enhance that fellowship and make it a reality to those who as yet have never experienced it. Let us strive to help answer the prayer of Jesus offered long, long ago, "Father, I pray that they all may be one . . . that the world may believe that thou hast sent me." (cf. John 17:21).

The Household
Of God

by
Gene W. Newberry

Reprinted from *Christian Leadership,* January 1959.

IN THE successful play "Family Portrait," Mary, the mother of Jesus, is greatly distressed that she can make no sense out of the crucifixion of her son. Later in the play a baby is born to Mary's youngest son, Judah. Mary goes to Judah and timidly asks him to name the baby Jesus. Her reason is given in a memorable line: "I'd like him not to be forgotten."

Mary need not have worried about her Son being forgotten. His church was to become the community of memory. Although he said little about the church in a formal way, its establishment was the inevitable outcome of his work. "He ordained twelve, that they should be with him, and that he might send them forth to preach" (Mark 3:14). Thus he gathered around him a body of disciples which could not but expand and take on the form of a regular community. There (and now) we have the church where two or three are gathered in his name. Above all, he proclaimed the kingdom of God. His followers were those who broke with the present world and threw in their lot with the new order which was at hand.

If our concept of "what the church is" is adequate, it must take its rise from biblical sources. This is prior to all other considerations including theological speculation and sociological inquiry. Notice the great clue given in both Old and New Testaments. The church is essentially a people, a religious community. The whole Bible is concerned with the distinct society called "the people of God." We see a continuity of meaning and saving work between the Christian church and Israel. Is it not helpful, then, to think of the church as founded upon God's covenant with Israel, and refounded upon Christ's sacrificial life and death?

This truth adds depth to our doctrine of the church. It shows that it has been God's plan from the beginning to make those who were no people a people for his name. God's work with Israel was revealing and redemptive action. In the new Israel it has been extended universally. In Christ, therefore, the church has its decisive reconstituting and sealing. A further impressive stage was the church's inaugural and indwelling by the Holy Spirit at Pentecost. In very truth it is the presence of the Holy Spirit that constitutes and defines the church in its present meaning.

In the Book of Acts and the Epistles, the church is the whole household of the new people of God. There are local "outcroppings" of the universal family. Christ is the head and door of entrance. Paul addresses his first letter to Corinth "to those . . . called to be saints together with all those who in every place call on the name of our Lord Jesus Christ, both their Lord and ours" (1:2). It is a mistake to think that Christians formed local churches which federated into one great church. Rather, every new Christian became a member of the already existing community having its beginning in Christ and continuous with the concept of the people of God in the Old Testament.

Definition and mission go together and help define each other. To put them together will relate the church properly to Christ and his saving work.

Let us ask, for example, what kind of thinking pattern we follow when our mind turns to the concept of the church in our time. Do we think of it as a hospital or sanatorium? a school? an army? or something more heavenly, like the New Jerusalem? Perhaps we have used all of these analogies helpfully at one time or another, for all of them together do not exhaust the biblical meaning of the church.

A Time to Remember: TEACHINGS

The church is a hospital ministering to the health and healing of people. This is a very appealing picture for, at some time or other, all are overtaken by physical, mental, or spiritual sickness. Nothing is more characteristic of our time.

The church is a school with Christ. All of us, young and old, live and learn at his feet, imbibe of his spirit, are instructed and nurtured by his truth. The fellowship of the household of God is a lifelong educative activity.

Some, especially the young, find the picture of the church as an army most challenging. The heroic Christ distresses the comfortable, and brings not always peace. We are soldiers, gird for battle, crusading for truth and right, using the church as our beachhead in enemy-held territory.

We must not forget that the church also calls people to the New Jerusalem, the home of the soul. We are a ''goal people'' on a pilgrimage, with a dream in our eye and hope in our soul. The church at her best keeps our finest dreams and hopes from dying.

A mountaineer sat in front of the village store with a piece of wood and a sharp knife in his hands carving a horse. A tourist intrigued by his skill asked how he did it. The mountaineer's response was that he simply whittled away ''all that ain't horse.'' Some of us have the suspicion that many things can attach themselves to the church that are not essential to her true nature and work. The big question is whether we can recover those primary meanings about the household of God and thereby ''let the church be the church'' again. A half-dozen affirmations concern us: membership, ministry, structure, mission, worship, and message.

Membership. We affirm the inseparability of two truths and two experiences—that of becoming a Christian and of becoming a member of the fellowship. We are made members of Christ and of each other. Furthermore, God sets the bounds of the community of believers. It is the gathered group, the collected community.

Ministry. We affirm that there is no warrant in scripture for priestly mediation and authority. All are laymen alike. All are ministers alike. The challenge is to be each other's priest and to serve each other in Christlike love.

Structure. We affirm that the church, throughout her history, has been structured. She is no spooky, nebulous phantom. Think of the shepherd and the sheep, the vine and the branches. As the Body of Christ, the church has parts, functions, and activities.

Mission. We affirm that the church on earth is the church militant and combines the twin goals of reconciliation and service. Her purpose is to increase among men love of God and love of neighbor.

Worship. We affirm that man was made to respond to God's revelation and grace. The church accepts this relationship and, in her worship, appropriately and dramatically responds in adoration and participation. Worship then is the sublimest expression of fellowship with God.

Message. We affirm that formal, intellectual creeds have not been able to contain the good news of redemption—that God was in Christ reconciling the world unto himself. The dynamic message we proclaim is that of an authentic renewal of life and growth in God's grace.

Are these basic truths regarding the household of God biblical? Are they insightful? Are they practicable? We have been trying to say, with modesty and with thanksgiving, that they are. An acceptance of them and an application of them will assist the church in growing up to her true self, in becoming the church she was meant to be.

The Meaning and Mission
Of the Local Church
by
James E. Massey

Excerpted from *The Worshiping Church*, by James E. Massey (Anderson, Ind.: Warner Press, Inc., Copyright © 1961).

EACH local member should understand that the local congregation is not an end in itself, but rather that it is an extention of the older, wider church. The local church is not best explained as a collection formed by consenting wills but a Christian community brought about by the creative work of the Holy Spirit. The local church is a sphere of the saving activity of God in a given locale; it stands before the public as a "for instance," a point of evidence to show in concrete terms the result of the Christian message. It should be seen, then, that every member of such a community is to be a partner under God in a godly endeavor. The needs of the area are considered, and in the light of those considerations the worshiping, witnessing group should seek to represent God with the immediacy, drive, and decision that will honor the experience and claims that it asserts. With such a community of committed members, a local congregation will commend and not contradict the glories of the God to whom it is committed.

The difference between a congregation and "the church" is quite often misunderstood. In many cases it is given little regard. "The church," the body of Christ, is the community of the redeemed, indwelt and molded by the Spirit of God in the faith that exalts Jesus as Savior and Lord. Its expression is both local and worldwide.

The church has been described variously. The New Testament presents us with many descriptive figures that highlight definite aspects of its life in Christ. Paul described the church to the Ephesians as a *body* (1:23). The idea prominent here is that possession which Christ fills in the earth. Again to the Ephesians he wrote of the church as a *building:* "In whom all the building fitly framed together groweth unto an holy temple in the Lord: In whom ye also are builded together for an habitation of God through the Spirit" (2:21-22). Again a place of dwelling is the prominent idea. In Ephesians 5:25-32, the idea of the church as *bride* is set forth by Paul. The fact of promised fulfillment is the central feature in the picture there. Peter gave another angle of insight when he exhorted the Christians to "love the brotherhood" (1 Pet. 2:17b). The church is thus a *brotherhood*. Descriptions could be multiplied, but the instances would all highlight the fact that all believers in Christ are unified in a special sharing made possible through the Spirit of God. Every true Christian is positioned within the church as a "brother," "living stone," "member." The meaning is both spiritual and social in its depth and implications. Oneness is central in every picture of the church.

A congregation should keep such meanings before its members. This is necessary in order to help the local group reflect what the church is, and to have recognized points of contact. There should be, first, the faith-inspiring, written Word of God. Second, every member of the local group should confess Jesus Christ as his personal Savior and Lord. Membership in the group should be predicated upon that fact. The congregation should regard itself as an extension of that wider fellowship which Jesus began and called "my church." A third point of contact is seen when the local, organized congregation keeps its social order a spiritually governed order. A local congregation is at its best when the vitality and vision of the church are made evident in its life and witness.

It is on the local level of the congregation that the glory and beauty of the church is to be reflected. Ideally, every local fellowship should furnish a conspicuous example of what was originally invested in that early band of twelve that Jesus chose. It should be an obvious open evidence that God is at work in the midst of people. This is certainly possible for a local church when its members regard themselves as redeemed participants in an eternal purpose under God.

The local church is a fellowship of promise. The specialty of the group should be obedience to the will of God. It is to such an end that all attitudes, emotions, mental and material equipment should be directed. The promise of the group must be realized. Thus the need for the organizing of its work.

In its organized life a congregation will follow a pattern that is largely determined by group consent and scriptural principles. Organization can follow arbitrary patterns. There will no doubt be membership rules. There will be some stable forms to preserve continuity as one passing generation links with the oncoming generation. In some matters, human inventiveness will be seen as necessary in determining policies. Organized work must not be casual but causal. Every member of the church should be alert to let the spirit of the Lord operate in the lives of the persons who plan and carry on the work of the church.

The Apostolic Church
Our Standard
by
Charles E. Brown

Excerpted from *The Apostolic Church: A Study in Historical Theology,* by Charles E. Brown (Anderson, Ind.: Warner Press, Copyright © 1947).

THE WAY in which the apostolic church sets a normative standard for us today requires some thoughtful consideration. It is obvious that we do not have to imitate the apostolic church in every respect. As a boy, I well remember how my deep admiration for the apostolic church and its holy saints and ministers caused me to feel a secret yearning to wear the flowing robes and sandals of those holy men, and it was this deep admiration which drove me to seek to learn the language in which they first preached the Word of God. I regard this as an innocent manifestation of a passionate admiration for the men of the apostolic church.

Nevertheless, every intelligent person immediately perceives that it is not necessary for us to imitate the apostolic church in the clothing that we wear, nor in merely mechanical reproduction of the conditions of their physical life and work. However, we are under a most heavy responsibility, so far as possible, to reproduce the spiritual life, the truth, the doctrine, the holy equality of the universal priesthood of believers; the warm, rich, deep fellowship; and the burning message of redemption, as well as the overwhelming experiences of the Spirit's complete control of our lives.

Comparing the apostolic church with the corrupt Christianity of our times is like comparing a healthy baby with a fully mature man who is, nevertheless, badly crippled by diseases which deform and disfigure him and make his life a failure. Supposing that this deformed, diseased individual was once a normal healthy infant, then in order to regain his infantile estate it is not necessary for him to lose the wisdom and experience of the accumulated years. What he needs to do is return to the health of the infant, which is not exactly the same thing as becoming an infant again. He does not need to recover the ignorance and immaturity of childhood, but the health and normality of childhood. He does not seek for the undeveloped mind of the child, but for the condition of health and vigor of his early days. He seeks that the bent limbs may be straightened, that the stiff joints may be loosened.

This is a parable of what we mean by a return to or a restoration of the apostolic church. Such a reformation does not mean a restoration of all the conditions of life in apostolic times. We would not wear robes and sandals, speak the Aramaic language, or travel about on donkeys, or in horse-drawn chariots. We may even have a better administration of such matters as the Lord's Supper than the apostolic church had in Corinth, where "one is hungry, and another is drunken" (1 Cor. 11:21). We have no call to reproduce the abuses and weaknesses of the apostolic church, but whenever we reproduce its normal spirit and health we reach the ultimate height of blessedness in this time world.

Every congregation of Christian people which puts itself radically back on the basis of apostolic Christianity will find a wonderful upsurge of new, creative, spiritual power, which restores a certain childlike simplicity and freedom from snobbery, social emulation, and all the artificial distinctions of wealth, scholarship, and social standing. Such a congregation may contain scholars, scientists, and men with a vast grasp of affairs; but each of these will, as it were, instinctively, place himself on the level of the universal priesthood of believers and exercise his fellowship with the believers on the basis of spirituality and not that of any artificial human value.

What Does "Apostolic" Mean?

by
Harold W. Boyer

Excerpted from *The Apostolic Church and the Apostasy,*

by Harold W. Boyer (Anderson, Ind.: Warner Press, Copyright © 1960).

WHEN we use the term *apostolic* we mean that which was taught and established by the apostles. Thus, when we say apostolic teaching, preaching, practice, or church, we are claiming that the thing to which we attach the word *apostolic* is given to us directly from the apostles of our Lord Jesus.

The writer has some reservation about the term apostolic church, because I do not believe the apostles would have wanted the church to bear their names either individually or collectively. They preached Christ, and the collective body of believers who accepted him did not bear the name of the apostles, but the name of God. That early church was simply called the *ekklesia,* the church, or the church of God. Christ alone was recognized as the head of the church. Ephesians 1:22-23: "And hath put all things under his feet, and gave him to be the head over all things to the church, which is his body, the fullness of him that filleth all in all." Colossians 1:17-19: "And he is before all things, and by him all things consist. And he is the head of the body, the church: who is the beginning, the firstborn from the dead; that in all things he might have the preeminence. For it pleased the Father that in him should all fullness dwell." As worthy as the apostles are of all honor, when names are changed meanings shift with the change; to shift the emphasis in the name of the church from its rightful head will tend to shift also the allegiance of the people. Therefore, it is only because of the popular usage of the term and as a convenient historical designation that we use the word *apostolic* in this discourse.

With all respect to that early church, it is a bit wearisome to hear the uninformed speak of it as though it never had a fault, never a disagreement, and never a failure. Such was not the case. By way of illustration, hear the Apostle Paul as he wrote to the church at Galatia, "O foolish Galatians, who hath bewitched you, that ye should not obey the truth.

. . . Are ye so foolish? having begun in the Spirit, are ye now made perfect by the flesh?'' (Gal. 3:1-3). Hear the same apostle as he wrote to the church at Corinth, ''For it hath been declared unto me of you, my brethren, . . . that there are contentions among you'' (1 Cor. 1:11).

We must not comfort ourselves in our shortcomings by the knowledge that such conditions as these existed in the early church. They were wrong then! They are ten times worse now! The early church did not have the New Testament. The church was young, and it was persecuted. To be a Christian was to risk your very life. In most instances that early church walked in all the light it had. But the church today is nearly two thousand years old, and it has both the New Testament and the full presence of the promised Holy Spirit. Therefore, it should do much better than the early church was capable of doing. If this seems to cast any reflection on the early church, remember the words of our Lord who said of his own works, ''Verily, verily, I say unto you, He that believeth on me, the works that I do shall he do also; and greater works than these shall he do; because I go unto my Father'' (John 14:12).

We will do well to remember the background of the early church. It was composed of converted Jews and converted pagans whose backgrounds were worlds apart. Christianity was in the making. The New Testament was in the process of being written, but it would be many years before these scattered writings would be assembled into one book and recognized as the New Testament of God to man. It was impossible for the early church to be perfect either in theology or action. It is never safe to judge your fellowman by his actions; he may not know any better. It is never safe to judge him by his theology; his heart might be right even though his theology is wrong. It is always safe to follow the scriptural injunction, ''Judge not, that ye be not judged. For with what judgment ye judge, ye shall be judged: and with what measure ye mete, it shall be measured to you again'' (Matt. 7:1-2).

We cannot become a perfect church by comparing ourselves with the so-called apostolic church; it, too, has many imperfections. We can find ourselves only by searching the Bible which sets forth God's perfect plan for his church. In all our strivings we should not have as our goal or model the so-called apostolic church; rather we should look to the plan God set forth for his church in the New Testament. A church that recognizes Christ alone as its head and the Holy Spirit as its governor is patterning after the New Testament standard. If I compare myself with John Wesley, Daniel S. Warner, or some other great Christian, I do not see myself as I ought. We must see ourselves as compared with our Lord. The same is true of the church.

The early church did not have much that could be seen. Often she had no church house. She had no New Testament. We are impelled to inquire, What did she have?

She had an experience. Her people knew "old things are passed away; behold, all things are become new" (2 Cor. 5:17). They forsook sin. They knew they were born anew. They knew they were sanctified, because the abiding power and presence of the Holy Ghost kept them holy and filled with power. Their power did not lie in nor depend upon people or things. Their power flowed from their inner experience with God. We honestly believe that this same old-fashioned experience of full salvation will produce the same kind of church today. It will take away man's lust for pleasure. It will take away his timid fear of men and devils. It will take away his yen to argue theology. It will give him a holy zeal and power to fill the world with the gospel. It will give him the ability to win souls for Christ. How profound the words of Jesus, "Out of the abundance of the heart the mouth speaketh" (Matt. 12:34).

Not only did the early church have an experience with God, but she also had stalwart courage—courage that amounted to holy boldness. Her members openly declared, "We know that we have passed from death unto life" (1 John 3:14). They had no fear or worry for the flesh and did not seek reputation or the world's applause. "They loved not their lives unto the death" (Rev. 12:11). "They . . .

went everywhere preaching the gospel'' (Acts 8:4). They declared with John, "We know that we are of God, and the whole world lieth in wickedness" (1 John 5:19). There was romance and daring in the heart of the early church; she was filled with the warm glow of spiritual life and vigor.

If the church would go to her knees again, she would arise a witnessing church with power. So long as the church only grovels in the maze of her programs, bows to the opinions and authority of men, strives merely to attain a place of respectability with Babylon, she will remain powerless and anemic. She cannot rise to the standards of the New Testament while struggling with world mammon.

The members of the early church saw that every man was a prospect for Christ, and the church lost herself in an unselfish effort to share with all men what they had found in Jesus Christ. The church was highly successful because she did not put her trust entirely in human skills. Neither did her constituents appeal to civil authority; "they overcame by the blood of the Lamb, and by the word of their testimony" (Rev. 12:11).

To be a congregation that reaches the New Testament standard, we must have full salvation. By full salvation we mean to be saved and sanctified. We must have courage. We are not here to please ourselves, but to serve God. We must have faith and walk in the faith day by day. We do not light a candle to put under a bushel; neither does God want a church whose activities never go from under the roof of its building.

Where does my church stand in the light of the New Testament church? The only way I can answer that is by answering the question, Where do *I* stand in the light of Jesus Christ? Have I been born anew? Have I received the Holy Spirit? Am I living a holy, spirit-filled life? Am I spiritually alive or just a dead weight doing more to hinder the ongoing program of God than to help it?

Clarifying
Church Authority
by
Boyce W. Blackwelder

Excerpted from *Light From the Greek New Testament,* by
Boyce W. Blackwelder (Anderson, Ind.: Warner Press,
Copyright © 1958).

AN AWARENESS of the distinction between *petros* and
petra clears away difficulties of interpretation in Matthew
16:18. Some expositors, faced with a problem in verses
17-19 have questioned the genuineness of the passage. But
such an approach does not come to grips with the main
issue. There is no textual evidence that the verses in question are an interpolation, hence no reason for doubting their
authenticity.

An understanding of the distinction generally observed in
Koine Greek between *petra,* a massive rock, and *petros,* a
detached rock or stone, makes the words of Jesus clear. If it
be argued that Jesus probably spoke Aramaic in the conversation with Peter, and that Aramaic makes no such distinction between the terms, it can be stated that the writer of
the New Testament account understood a distinction and
expressed it by the two different words.

There are several strong arguments which show that
Peter (*petros*) and the rock (*petra*) upon which the church is
built are not identical. All the pronouns in Matthew 16:18
are emphatic, contrasting the person of Peter with the
mighty rock which is the foundation of the church. The
different genders (*petros,* masculine; and *petra,* feminine)
emphasize a distinction in the references.

Since *petra* is used metaphorically several times to indicate Christ (Rom. 9:33; 1 Cor. 10:4; 1 Pet. 2:8), it is in harmony with the Scriptures to take it thus in Matthew 16:18. In this light Jesus means that *he* is the foundation of the church. He speaks of himself as the builder, and uses the expression "my church." So the New Testament *ekklesia* is built upon Christ's deity and Saviorhood, upon the efficacy of his blood, and upon the immutability and objectivity of truth. It is obvious that no human being could be the support of such a structure.

The church is the creative work of God. Actually Peter's confession was impossible apart from the divine revelation upon which his proclamation was based. Jesus makes this point clear in Matthew 16:17. This revelation was not disclosed to Peter only. It was also the experience of the other disciples, and it is the impetus which makes possible the confession of any and all believers now as then. The church is based upon the truth which Peter confessed, that is, upon the reality that Jesus is the Christ, the Son of the living God. In verse 18 our Lord is also in effect saying to Simon, "The power of the gospel which has transformed you into a man of dependable character [implied in *petros*] will likewise change other persons, and as a result of this redemption the church is build." Thus we see that the church never produces salvation; salvation produces the church.

There is a sense in which the inspired writings and work of all the apostles and prophets have their place in the divine plan of the church of which Jesus Christ is the cornerstone (Eph. 2:20). In fact, all believers are living stones *(lithoi)* in God's temple (1 Pet. 2:5). But Peter has no special position or prerogative above the other apostles. Nowhere in the New Testament is any supremacy assigned to him.

Misunderstanding in much of Christendom has long been associated with Jesus' words about binding and loosing in Matthew 16:19 and 18:18. The participles in those passages have been traditionally rendered as though they were simple futures, viz., "shall be bound . . . shall be loosed" (King James, English Revised, American Standard, Revised Standard, Confraternity; same idea in Weymouth, Moffatt, Montgomery, Goodspeed, and others).

But these participles are not simple future verbs. They are future perfect passive participles, and in light of this, the translation of Matthew 16:19 would go like this: "I will give you [singular] the keys of the kingdom of heaven, *but* whatever *you may bind* [*deseis,* aorist active subjunctive] on earth *shall have been bound* [*estai dedemenon,* periphrastic future perfect passive] in heaven, and whatever *you may loose* [*luseis,* aorist active subjunctive] on earth *shall have been loosed* [*estai* periphrastic future perfect passive] *in heaven.*

Likewise the translation of Matthew 18:18 is: "Verily I say to you [plural personal pronoun], whatsoever you may *bind* [*desete,* aorist active subjunctive] upon earth *shall have been bound* [*estai dedemena,* periphrastic future perfect passive] in heaven, and whatsoever *you may loose* [*lusete,* aorist active subjunctive] upon earth *shall have been loosed* [*estai lelumena,* periphrastic future perfect passive] in heaven.

Thus Matthew 16:19 and 18:18 are seen to be in harmony with the general tenor of the New Testament which nowhere teaches sacerdotalism. "Binding" and "loosing" are used metaphorically of course, in the passages, meaning "prohibiting" and "permitting." All that is proclaimed by the ministry and church must be based on the Lord's authority.

Professor Mantey has pointed out that Matthew 16:19 and 18:18 were rendered incorrectly in the Latin Vulgate Version by Jerome about A.D. 400. Concerning that regrettable error, Dr. Mantey adds: "No doubt millions of people have been misled by believing their sins were forgiven by God, when some religious leader had pronounced their sins forgiven, in spite of the fact that they had not met the conditions of God's forgiveness."

There are serious theological implications in the traditional rendering. Has any religious communion or its clergy been authorized by the Lord Jesus Christ to remit or to retain men's sins? Has any ecclesiastical body the prerogative to impart salvation in God's behalf? Can any institution or its representatives make pronouncements which heaven is bound to ratify? If the common rendering of the passages in question is true, disciples on earth are given authority over heaven! But is not the converse true? Does not the general tenor of the New Testament indicate that heaven is our authority and that God determines the policy of the ministry and church? According to the Scriptures, it is the function of the clergy to set forth the terms of salvation, making known what God has declared. Man is only the servant or ambassador of the Almighty. God is sovereign, and gives to no human being the prerogative of pronouncing the salvation or the damnation of any soul. Clergymen, therefore, are not judges who decide the destinies of their hearers. They are proclaimers of salvation on divine terms.

The two verses under consideration, as traditionally rendered and interpreted, are strongholds for advocates of sacerdotalism. What are the implications of the Greek tenses in these passages?

The phrases commonly rendered "shall be bound . . . shall be loosed" are not simple future tenses, but are periphrastic future perfect passive participles. They should be translated as such, and the interpreter should bring forth the total idea conveyed by such a construction. The same participles and constructions are found in both passages, the only difference being that in Matthew 16:19 the participles are singular because Peter is addressed, while in 18:18 the participles are plural because the group of disciples is addressed.

It is precarious to treat these participles as though they were simple futures and give them a figurative or irregular rendering. There should be no interpretative problem regarding the tense of the participles. If the Greek writer wished to convey the thought expressed by the simple future, why did he not use that tense? Had he desired to express the idea conveyed by the present or simple future, those forms were at his disposal. We must assume that because of the significance of the perfect, that was the tense the Greek writer wished to use to express precisely what he had in mind.

The Name of the Church
by
Floyd W. Heinly

Reprinted from *Yearbook of the Church of God: 1923,* ed. by John A. Morrison (Anderson, Ind.: Gospel Trumpet Company, 1923).

WHEN our new mission-house was opened in Kuringram, Bengal, India, one of the first tasks that was ours was to hang out the signboard. As I looked at it immediately after Brother Khan had put it in place, and read "Church of God," I felt a decidedly greater thrill of joy at the beauty of the name than I ever had felt before. For I saw the name while in a new atmosphere.

Here we were surrounded, not by indoctrinated Christians, but by Hindus and Mohammedans. The latter, in their zeal for Mohammed, are bitter against Christ. A sign-board announcing "Church of Christ" would have been an eyesore to them. But Mohammedan and Hindu alike bow before the name "God." That name includes the three in one—Father, Son, and Holy Spirit. No name can be greater. And as I stood and looked and thought, I could see in that name a most captivating universality, a most appealing wisdom. Who could have found a better name than that to apply to the disciples of God's Son?

What is there in a name? Many say it makes no difference by what name a body of Christians is called. But compare the following names: "Church of England," "Church of Scotland," "Church of Rome," "Church of God." Who would for a moment hesitate to prefer the last? An Oriental man cannot understand national and sectional names applied to Christian churches, such as Eastern, Western, American, North, South; nor names that emphasize particular doctrines or forms of government, such as Seventh-day Adventist, Holiness, Pentecostal, Baptist, Episcopal, Presbyterian, Congregational. And much less can he appreciate men's names, as Lutheran, Wesleyan, Mennonite. But he readily understands why the name of God should be worthy of the most prominence, and why it should appear in the name applied to Christian disciples. The name of God appeals to the Oriental, but the Westerner seems to have studied to keep it out of the Church titles.

Many think it sounds too haughty to call a body "Church of God"—too much as though it means to say, "We are it—all of it." Wherever such haughtiness exists, it needs severe reproof and extinction. The name must be regarded with becoming humility. "Thou shalt not take the name of the Lord thy God in vain; for the Lord will not hold him guiltless that taketh his name in vain" (Exod. 20:7). This command comes next after the ones prohibiting idolatry, implying how closely such vanity is associated in God's mind with outright heathenism. I have no doubt that many congregations are, in principle, out of accord with the third commandment of the Decalog by calling themselves "church of God." They have "a name that they live, but are dead." But such misuse is no argument against right use.

Is there really nothing in a name? Is it of no weight that the apostles of Jesus Christ, particularly the one who once wasted the church of God, should so frequently call it by that name? Is it all the same whether a thing is called a man or an angel? Has not each name certain associations, and are not these brought before us immediately the word is spoken? Can "Church of Rome," or any other such national, sectional, or doctrinal name ever bring to our minds those thrills of joy and those ideals of purity that are at once suggested by the "Church of God"? Is the name of the Almighty to be substituted by less important ones? Are we safe in going so far in the direction of idolatry by such substitutions?

But someone will say: "You are now speaking of ideals. We must be practical. Various bodies must be distinguished from one another, just as persons are separately named; and if we do not name them, they will acquire a name somehow. Since there are different bodies, there must be different names."

It must readily be admitted that the great name "Church of God" does not fit well when attached to the various denominations individually. That is doubtless why it is avoided by many. They would feel too guilty if they took it, knowing that they are too far from being in accord with what the name implies. And it must also be admitted that the name has suffered much at the hands of many who have adopted it but lived far from it. Both of these are sad admissions. What do they imply? That nominal Christianity, generally speaking, is in such a bad way that it is obliged to avoid the name "church of God," so bad that it cannot conscientiously and boldly adopt it, so divided that many names must be used in order to differentiate between the many bodies. We can admit that various bodies require to be variously named; but that admission only shows up the more sadly the present state of affairs. Why should it be necessary to have various names? Did God intend it to be so? Is this what Jesus prayed for, and died for—that we might all be separated?

Without doubt a reformation vision and message are needed in this age; a vision of real unity, and a forceful preaching of it. The result must be unity. And for such a unified body, no other name under heaven is so suitable, so universal, so inclusive of heaven as well as earth, so divine, so awe-inspiring, so love-begetting, so attractive to all men of all nations, Orientals and Occidentals, so widely known, as that in which God is given the preeminence of which he alone is worthy.

It may be objected to that no society or body will ever come up to such an ideal name; that even the early church did not rise to it. But the early church is our example only in so far as it came up to the ideals and standards of Christ. We are not to imitate its sins. Jesus himself threatened some of the congregation with complete removal from him if they did not repent. We are to preach the vision and the message, no matter who has failed, and no matter how far the present age may be from it. Only by persistently holding forth the ideal shall we be able to change the mind of this generation. And to say that no body of people will ever be worthy of the name "church of God" is to say that conditions must continue to be so bad that the name will not be applicable, and to admit that we have little faith in our message, if indeed we have a message at all. This is surrender; cowardly surrender!

If ever the increasing mass of heathenism is conquered for God, there must be an army that is worthy of the name "church of God." And being worthy, no one can object to the name.

The Nature
Of Church Ordinances
by
Russell R. Byrum

Excerpted from *Christian Theology: A Systematic Statement of Christian Doctrine for the Use of Theological Students,* by Russell R. Byrum (Anderson, Ind.: Gospel Trumpet Company, Copyright © 1925).

THE New Testament ordinances are certain divinely appointed outward observances which are significant of spiritual truths of the gospel. The Old Testament religion was one great system of outward ceremonies. These have been abolished. The Christian religion also has its symbolic rites, fewer and simpler than those given by Moses, but more expressive. Romanists hold a much larger number of ordinances than do most Protestants. Their ordinances, or sacraments as they call them, are seven in number—ordination, confirmation, matrimony, extreme unction, penance, baptism, and the eucharist. The first five of these are not properly classed with the two latter as ordinances. The criteria of an ordinance have been well described as, (1) An outward symbol divinely appointed to represent a great fact or truth of the gospel and the personal relation of the recipient to that fact or truth and (2) A divine requirement, making its obligation universal and perpetual. The first five sacraments of the Romish church as above named lack in whole or in part these criteria.

From an early date the ordinances were regarded as efficacious in actually conferring saving grace upon those who participated in them. This view has persisted to the present time, not only among Roman Catholics, but also in various Protestant communions. It is so represented in their statements of faith. But neither the Scriptures nor reason furnish any ground for supposing salvation may be obtained by any physical means. The common sense of mankind instinctively repudiates the idea that any magical efficacy exists in any outward rite that of itself can confer spiritual grace. But though the ordinances do not confer grace, yet they are evidently a *means* of grace. They are a means of grace in the same sense as is the preaching of the gospel. In the Christian ordinances God has set forth certain fundamental truths of religion. In the preaching of the gospel these truths are addressed to the ear, but in the ordinances they are represented to the eye in visible form by means of material symbols. Augustine well said, "A sacrament is the word of God made visible." As preaching is instrumental in salvation and spiritual edification, so are the ordinances. Because they are divinely given representations of certain central truths *of* Christianity, no variation in the form of their observance from that represented in the Scriptures is permissible. Any such perversion of the forms of the ordinances is as objectionable as to change the words of the Scriptures.

Identifying
The Ordinances
by
Earl L. Martin

Excerpted from *What a Christian Should Believe,* by Earl L. Martin (Anderson, Ind.: Gospel Trumpet Company, © 1928).

"IT IS ONLY an ordinance!" So say many people when we talk with them about baptism, the Lord's Supper, and foot washing. "Only an ordinance!" Indeed! Strange. Why, does not an ordinance signify something *ordained, appointed, decreed,* an observance *commanded?* But there are some who will not agree that baptism, the Lord's Supper, and foot washing, especially the last, are observances commanded. However, they are so set forth in God's Word. They are commanded, therefore should be observed, for Christ said, "Teaching them to observe all things whatsoever I have commanded you: and lo, I am with you alway, even unto the end of the world" (Matt. 28:20).

Baptism—It is an ordinance of the New Testament because it is an observance commanded. Christ, in his last great commission, said, "Go ye into all the world, and preach the gospel to every creature. He that believeth and is baptized shall be saved" (Mark 16:15-16).

Jesus, our great example, was baptized (see Matt. 3:13-17). Not only was he baptized, but he (through his disciples) baptized others. He enjoined baptism upon all believers, saying, "He that believeth and is baptized shall be saved." He instructed his apostles to preach it and to practice it. And they did. In the first sermon after Pentecost we hear Peter saying, "Repent, and be baptized every one of you in the name of Jesus Christ" (Acts 2:38). "Then they that gladly received his word were baptized: and the same day there were added unto them about three thousand souls" (v. 41).

Baptism is for believers. "He that believeth and is baptized"; "They that gladly received his word"; "Repent and be baptized"; "They were baptized, both men and women" (Acts 8:12). It is sometimes argued, in support of infant baptism, that the apostles baptized infants, for it says that they baptized households. But where is the proof that there were infants in these households? If you will read the accounts (Acts 10 and 16:31-34) you will see that the households believed. Children under the age of accountability cannot repent, nor are they capable of believing; therefore they are not eligible for baptism. Being baptized in infancy will not make one a Christian. "Ye must be born again." Then you may be scripturally baptized.

As to the mode. Immersion is the uniform teaching of the Word. The very word "baptize" means to "immerse, plunge, or dip." Baptism, according to the Scriptures, is "*in water.*" Immersion alone expresses the significance of baptism. Baptism is an outward testimony to an inward work of grace. Christians have died to sin and have been resurrected to walk in newness of life. Baptism is represented as a burial. "Therefore we are buried with him by baptism into death: that like as Christ was raised up from the dead by the glory of the Father, even so we also should walk in newness of life'' (Rom. 6:4). Sprinkling or pouring cannot represent a burial. Baptism is a burial in water.

Baptism does not actually save us. It does not literally wash away our sins. Only the blood of Christ can do that. It is a ceremonial cleansing, ''the answer of a good conscience toward God.'' But let this lead no one to say that since baptism does not actually save us, they do not need to be baptized. While it is true that we are not saved merely by being baptized, it is also true that we can only be saved as we are willing to obey, and this includes obedience in being baptized.

The Lord's Supper—It is on this wise: ''As they were eating [Christ and his disciples] Jesus took bread, and blessed it, and brake it, and gave it to the disciples, and said, Take, eat; this is my body. And he took the cup, and gave thanks, and gave it to them, saying, Drink ye all of it; for this is my blood of the new testament, which is shed for many for the remission of sins'' (Matt. 26:26-28). So it was instituted and its observance commanded by Christ. In obedience to his command and following his example we find the early church observing this ordinance. ''They continued steadfastly in the apostles' doctrine and fellowship, and in breaking of bread, and in prayers'' (Acts 2:42). Paul delivered it to the churches to which he preached, and they observed it: ''For I have received of the Lord that which also I delivered unto you, that the Lord Jesus the same night in which he was betrayed took bread, etc.'' (1 Cor. 11:23-26). They observed it, for ''the disciples came together to break bread'' (Acts 20:7). Its observance is commanded, ''till he come.''

It, too, like baptism, is a ceremony. It has a deeply spiritual significance. ''This do in remembrance of me'' (Luke 22:19), said Christ. It is in memory of Christ. It points backward to Calvary, where his body was broken and his blood was shed for us. The bread is a symbol of that broken body, and the wine an emblem of that shed blood. It is for all those who discern the body of Christ. In it we "do show the Lord's death till he come" (1 Cor. 11:26). We are not given any definite rules as to the frequency or the time of its observance. The Scripture simply says, "As oft as ye drink it."

Foot Washing—This, too, the same as baptism and the Lord's Supper, was instituted and its observance commanded by Christ. First, he gave us an example of it (read John 13). That Christ literally washed the disciples' feet is beyond argument. And we cannot better explain it than by emphasizing what he did and what he said.

Note first his insistence upon it: "If I wash thee not, thou hast no part with me" (v. 8). Thus he made it obligatory upon Peter. Now read verses 12-17: "So after he had washed their feet, and had taken his garments, and was set down again, he said unto them, Know ye what I have done unto you? Ye call me Master and Lord: and ye say well; for so I am. If I then, your Lord and Master, have washed your feet; ye also ought to wash one another's feet. For I have given you an example, that ye should do as I have done to you. Verily, verily, I say unto you, The servant is not greater than his lord; neither he that is sent greater than he that sent him. If ye know these things, happy are ye if ye do them."

He gave us an example. What is an example for but to follow? He said we *ought* to do it. The word *ought* means "duty bound." We are under direct obligation. He promised a blessing if we should do it. "Happy are ye if ye do them." "These things" and "them" refer to the Lord's Supper, which he had instituted that very same evening, and foot washing, which he was then instituting, and which observance he was then commanding.

The fact that it has not been as generally observed as the other ordinances proves nothing against it. It simply proves that men have not had all the light. It has been argued against, but every argument that has been used against it could be used with equal force against baptism and the

Lord's Supper. "It was an old custom," says someone. So were bathing and eating. But Jesus gave them a deeply spiritual meaning in his ordinances. Foot washing is a symbol of what our attitude should be toward all our brethren in the Lord. This, as well as all other things, can be done "decently and in order." The argument cannot be used against it that it is an impropriety. It can easily be managed so its practice will be becoming, with the men in one room, the women in another, men washing the feet of the men, and women of the women.

The correct Christian attitude should be one of belief and acceptance of all the teachings of Christ, instead of an endeavor to deny or explain them away.

Paul praised the Corinthians that they had kept the ordinances as he had given them to them. This should be to the praise of every Christian. "If ye know these things, happy are ye if ye do them."

The One Essential
Of Christian Unity

by
Robert L. Berry

Excerpted from *The Holy Spirit*, by Robert Lee Berry, (Anderson, Ind.: Warner Press, Copyright © 1932).

UNLESS the Spirit of God gets a chance at this great problem it never will be solved. The church, being of the nature that it is, and the Holy Spirit being the one animating, life-giving spirit of the church, it is only reasonable and logical that he knows the way to unity.

We infer that he would begin with the individual as he always does and begin with his heart. From the nature of the work of the Spirit we are led to believe that he would begin with causing all Christians to love one another fervently.

We could believe that the Holy Spirit would create in all Christians one great big overwhelming, propulsive purpose, one so big, so dominating, that all other purposes would bend to that one. And that purpose, we should think, would be to carry the whole gospel to the whole world.

Then he would rally all men around Jesus, the magnet of all souls, the Star of Hope, the great Head of the church, who in his high priestly prayer made intercession for the unity of his people. He said: "Neither pray I for these alone, but for them also which shall believe on me through their word; that they all may be one; as thou, Father, art in me, and I in thee, that they also may be one in us: that the world may believe that thou hast sent me" (John 17:20-21).

Just before this he had said, "Sanctify them through thy truth: thy word is truth. As thou hast sent me into the world, even so have I also sent them into the world. And for their sakes I sanctify myself, that they also might be sanctified through the truth" (John 17:17-19).

We could expect the Holy Spirit to bring purity to the church, to every scattered member of the body; for purity is part of unity. The Holy Spirit would unite the whole body in one great consecration at the altar of God, where everyone would lay down his pet ideas, his very life and soul, and swing out free and only for Christ. The Holy Spirit would first baptize each one with himself and with fire, burning out all the selfish dross and creating a people with one heart and one soul. This cannot be done as long as one selfish cherished treasure is held to. All, all, must be yielded to the will of God.

We could expect the Holy Spirit to create the desire for unity in all hearts until there would arise a prayer, like the prayer of Jesus, from the depth of the heart, for God to bring together in one his scattered people. When this desire is created and this prayer is prayed God will show the way for its achievement. This we cannot doubt.

But one thing yet remains that is very important, which is, the Holy Spirit evidently waits to give the children of God a vision of how unity may be achieved. Of this we feel certain. There is the divine conviction that he knows the way, the actual steps to take, and that he only awaits the necessary humility and open-heartedness of God's children to show all of them the same identical steps to take.

But suppose all will not give the Holy Spirit the opportunity to reveal to them the secret of unity and mark out the road to it; what then?

Ah, the Holy Spirit never hesitates. He never waits on the masses. He works with the individual soul. Therefore, wherever he finds a soul willing to follow him all the way back to unity he shows that soul the way. Could he do otherwise? He could not. Does he wait to save all souls before he saves the one who yields? No. He saves that one. Does he wait to fill all believers before he fills the one believer who comes consecrating? No. He fills that one believer. The one Christian, who, deploring the divisions in the church, comes seeking the way to it, finds the solution. Does the Holy Spirit wait until all Christians come seeking that unity? No. He at once shows the way and leads that one Christian into unity.

The unity of the Spirit is the one essential of Christian unity. There is its beginning. Are we bold enough to believe that the Holy Spirit is a good enough teacher to reveal truth alike to the children of God? We are bold enough to believe that and courageous enough to submit the proposition that when God's children take him as the Teacher of truth that he will lead all into the same truth.

The theological seminaries never will bring unity. They could help immensely by teaching it, however. The human brain is too dense to see or know the way. Men cannot be indoctrinated into unity, and doctrine is essential. But men could be fused into Christian unity in the burning love of God. And the Holy Spirit will, if he is trusted, lead all into the truth, and while he is doing that he can keep the hearts all together.

We feel sure, also, that the Holy Spirit would appeal to the Scriptures for a basis of unity. He would bring us to their simplicity and to accept them as the last word. That is a basis for unity—when the Word is accepted as indeed the Word of God.

Let us, then, yield unto the Holy Spirit. He knows the way back to Christian unity, and he alone knows the way. All men's plans have failed or will fail from the very nature of the case. But if our holy religion is based on Christ, and the Holy Spirit has been sent to guide into truth and to animate one body, and since he knows the mind of Christ, surely he can accomplish the humanly impossible thing of bringing again Christian unity. Many are taking his way and are enjoying once more the unity of Pentecost. There is a new Pentecost!

A Basis
For Christian Unity
by
W. Dale Oldham

Reprinted from the *Gospel Trumpet*, June 28, 1947.

IN THE great prayer of Jesus recorded in John 17, the Master is pleading with his heavenly Father for the unity of his disciples. His plea was to the end that they all might be one. Jesus was interested not only in the forgiveness of sin, but also in the uniting and strengthening of the little body of believers. In this seventeenth chapter of John two essentials are stressed: the purification of the church through the reception of the Holy Spirit, and the uniting of the church through a common experience and a possessing love. However, Jesus was not praying only for the group which was then his little body of followers. He was praying for oneness to be manifested among *all* Christians.

Jesus planned for his followers to be one, and today he is still requiring that they be one. Listen to verses 20-21: "Neither pray I for these alone, but for them also which shall believe on me through their word; that they all may be one; as thou, Father, art in me, and I in thee, that they also may be one in us: that the world may believe that thou hast sent me." This quest for the unity of the church is reflected in words spoken by Paul to the church at Ephesus. In Ephesians 1, Paul states that God "having made known unto us the mystery of his will . . . that in the dispensation of the fullness of times might gather together in one all things in Christ, both which are in heaven, and which are on earth," (vv. 9-10). In John 10:16 Jesus said, "Other sheep I have, which are not of this fold; them also must I bring, and they shall hear my voice; and there shall be one fold, and one shepherd."

There seems to have been no need for more than one church in the early Christian era. There was not a church for the rich man and another for the poor man, a church for the highly educated and another for the illiterate, but all were able to share a common fellowship because they shared a common Christ who had provided a common experience of redemption for them all. Of that early morning church it was said, "They were all with one accord," (Acts 2:1). In Acts 4:32 we read, "And the multitude of them that believed were of one heart and of one soul." In those days the prayer of Christ for the unity of his followers was being fulfilled. What was true then can be visibly true today also if the same spirit comes to possess Christians now as possessed them nineteen centuries ago.

Division among God's people has always brought censure and condemnation for the Word of God. In 1 Corinthians 1:10 we read, "That there be no divisions among you." And in 1 Corinthians 12:25; "That there should be no schism [division] in the body." The body referred to is the body of Christ, or the church. Paul was constantly vocal in his condemnation of division in the church. When he found division in the church at Corinth he said that its cause was carnality. He said that variance and heresies and division were works of the flesh and not works of the Spirit. In Romans 16:17-18 Paul said, "I beseech you, brethren, mark them which cause divisions and offenses contrary to the doctrine which ye have learned; and avoid them. For they that are such serve not our Lord Jesus Christ."

Division among Christians is as bad in one place as it is in another. Division, rivalry, trouble, suspicion, heresy, lack of confidence, clannishness, are just as severely condemned among Christians today as they were among Christians in Paul's day; they are as severely condemned in one body of people as in another. To profess to be Christians and then tolerate such unchristian attitudes means for us to fall under the disapproval and the judgment of God. In Romans 2:1-2 we read, "Therefore thou art inexcusable, O man, whosoever thou art that judgest: for wherein thou judgest doest the same things. But we are sure that the judgment of God is according to truth against them which commit such things."

Spiritual disunity is condemned by the New Testament, whether it be in evidence in the larger body of Christendom or in the local congregation. Christian unity has three phases: it is international in its scope, it is congregational in its scope, but it is also a personal matter. Each Christian, as Paul informed the church at Ephesus, is under definite obligation to "endeavor to keep the unity of the spirit in the bonds of peace." Christian unity must become more than a theory; it must become the common practice of the church. It must become more than an ideal; it must become a reality.

We want in our generation a visible demonstration of Christian unity. We do not seek an absolute uniformity but we do seek a workable basis for Christian brotherhood and Christian unity. Paul in speaking on this subject did not demand an absolute accord in matters of conscience. In Romans 14:2-3 he said, "One believeth that he may eat all things: another, who is weak, eateth herbs. Let not him that eateth despise him that eateth not; and let not him which eateth not judge him that eateth; for God hath received him." And later on in the chapter he said, "One man esteemeth one day above another: another esteemeth every day alike. Let every man be fully persuaded in his own mind. He that regardeth the day regardeth it unto the Lord; and he that regardeth not the day, to the Lord he doth not regard it. He that eateth, eateth to the Lord, for he giveth God thanks; and he that eateth not, to the Lord he eateth not, and giveth God thanks," (vv.5-6). And in the tenth verse: "But why dost thou judge thy brother? or why dost thou set at naught thy brother? for we shall stand before the judgement seat of Christ." And in verse thirteen: "Let us not therefore judge one another any more: but judge this rather, than no man put a stumbling block or an occasion to fall in his brother's way."

The time will never come when all Christians will have the same opinions with regard to the methods and details involved in carrying out all phases of the work of the Kingdom. Such uniformity is not only unnecessary but in some cases is even undesirable. The detailed methods used in a large city church could not possibly be the same as would be used in carrying out mission work in the heart of darkest Africa. There was a time in the ministry of Paul when he differed radically with Barnabas in the matter of John Mark. Paul and Peter could not see eye to eye on every single matter presenting itself for their consideration, yet Paul made no attempt to excommunicate Barnabas and Peter. When James and the Jerusalem group differed with Paul those differences were submerged and were not permitted to break the fellowship of the brethren. If we humans, of whom the church is composed, were all omniscient and infallible and thus free from all error, there would be made possible a type of Christian unity which has never been found on earth. However, there is a Christian unity of the spirit, a vital blending of the hearts of Christian believers which is perfectly possible and desirable in spite of the fact that we are not infallible and we are not omniscient.

For some three years Jesus carefully taught his disciples in those matters pertaining to his doctrine and to his kingdom, and yet at the expiration of that period, most of them were woefully lacking in understanding. Christians today are standing at all stages in this matter comprehending the doctrine, the mind and the will of Jesus Christ. And yet, in conversion, every twice-born Christian enters into an experience so basic and life-changing—so broad and all-inclusive—that it instantly, through the power of Jesus Christ, makes him a brother to all other Christians in the whole wide world and even to the group of the redeemed in heaven.

The brotherhood of all Christian believers depends not upon the fact of God being the creator of our bodies, but upon the fact of Jesus Christ being our re-creator, our Savior, our deliverer from sin. Full fellowship does not depend upon comprehension of all truth. Just before his death Jesus said to his disciples, "I have many things to say to you, but ye cannot bear them now." The revelation of truth to the hearts of men is a gradual process, yet Christian fellowship and unity should be experienced instantly when the spirit of man is changed through conversion. Christian unity does not consist in complete uniformity in conscience matters or in the practices of public worship. Its basis is rather in the new birth, in men coming to that experience in which "old things pass away and all things become new."

Thus Christ becomes the true basis for Christian unity—not Christ as an historical figure, nor Christ as the head of a nominally Christian movement, but Christ as man's personal savior. There will never be complete unity among all the people who attend our churches, but there should be and must be a perfect Christian unity between all those who share a full conversion experience.

Let me again remind you of the words of Jesus, "I pray that they all may be one." Is that prayer too idealistic for a day like this? Is it beyond the realm of possibility? Or does Jesus really expect all Christians to be one? All genuinely converted men and women have common ground in Jesus Christ. They are all of the same family—not half-brothers and half-sisters, but full brothers and sisters in the Lord. Whenever we permit denominational insistences, creeds, clannishness, or anything else to separate us or cut us off from other groups of God's people, we thus cut ourselves off from the prayer of Jesus. If we as Christians will approach this problem with the same determination and persistence as that used by the scientists in perfecting the atomic bomb, we will be simply amazed at the progress which can be made along this line. Let us stand for truth and for principle. Let bigotry be thrown down and humility placed upon the throne. When Christ fully rules his church, his church will be one.

Jesus Prayed for Unity
by
Boyce W. Blackwelder

Reprinted from *Vital Christianity,* April 10, 1966. All Scripture quotes are given in Dr. Blackwelder's own translation.

THE SOLEMN WORDS which Jesus addressed to the Father on the evening before the Crucifixion constitute the longest of his recorded prayers and gives us an insight into how he views his ministry (John 17). His chief concern is for the salvation of the world, and within this soteriological framework his supplication is voiced. In verses 20-26, he emphasizes evangelism in terms of the integral witness of his followers, and his emphasis points up the basic features of the oneness of Christians. Thus we note:

1. **The Scope of the Oneness.** Jesus prays not only "for these" (the disciples who are at his side), but "for them also which shall believe on me through their word" (all future disciples, v. 20), "that they all may go on being one" (v. 21). Consequently his plea reaches out in ever-widening circles and embraces all Christians from the first century until the end of time.

2. **The Sphere of the Oneness.** According to Jesus' words the oneness of believers is "in us" (in the Father and the Son, v. 21). John 17:20-26 is cited often by persons who seek to promote the union of denominations, but external alliance does not seem to be suggested by the thought of the passage. The sphere of oneness transcends all outward structures.

3. **The Dynamic of the Oneness.** The power which unifies believers in the common spiritual life which is operative in everyone who knows God by faith in Jesus Christ. In verse 23, Jesus says, "I in them, and thou in me, that they may continue in the state of having been brought completely into oneness." Believers are one with each other because they are one with God. This spiritual affinity, which is the foundation of all outward expressions of cooperation, reaches its highest potential when God's people are filled with the Holy Spirit (cf. Acts 2:41-47).

4. **The Archetype of the Oneness.** Jesus prays that all believers "may go on being one as we (are) one" (v. 22; cf. v. 21). Thus the original pattern for the oneness of Christians is the oneness of the Father and Jesus. The connotation of the adverb *kathos*, which may be translated "as," "even as," or "according as" (vv. 11, 21-22) is not identity (the essential oneness of the Godhead cannot be duplicated) but analogy (the oneness can be imitated). That is to say, the oneness enjoyed by believers resembles that which exists between the Father and the Son. The unity of believers finds its ideal and its motivating princi-

ples in a personal relationship of muture love like that which characterizes the Persons of the Trinity.

5. **The Objective of Oneness.** From the prayer of Jesus it is clear that Christian unity is not an end in itself, but is a means to the redemptive thrust of the church. Jesus' followers are to maintain a clear and consistent witness to him so that the world "may go on believing" (v. 21) and "may go on knowing" (v. 23) that the Father has sent him to be the Savior of mankind. This request began to be fulfilled through the ministry of the early church (Act 2:41, 47; 4:4, 32; 5:14; 6:1; 19:20), and every generation of Christians, following the example of the courageous witness given by the first disciples, must continue an aggressive program of evangelism.

6. **The Realization of Oneness.** Jesus does not pray that the disciples might get to be one, but he speaks of oneness as if it were already a fact. He asks that the disciples "may go on" being one (*osin,* present subjunctive, vv. 11, 21, 22, 23). Our Lord implies that the oneness enjoyed by his early followers is to be perpetuated in the history of the church. Thus believers are to be kept in the Father's name (v. 11), and they are to be faithful to God's word (vv. 6, 14; cf. 2 Tim. 2:2). The unity of the church is promoted by the teaching of the truth of the gospel. See Jude 3 for *pistis,* "faith," used in the objective sense of the doctrines which were once (*hapax,* "for all time") delivered to the saints.

To what extent may ecclesiastical organizations be involved in corporate expressions of Christian unity? Inasmuch as the aim of unity is not union but evangelism, the question ought to be faced in terms of the moral and spiritual needs of the world. Hence the foremost inquiry should be, What sort of expression will be most effective in bringing the peoples of the earth to knowledge of and trust in Jesus Christ as Savior and Lord? What kind of establishments or activities must be utilized or created if the church is to carry out the universal commission (Mark 16:15; Matt. 28:19-20; Luke 24:47; Acts 1:8)?

The New Testament gives no specific structural patterns for world evangelization, but from the early expansion of Christianity we note certain basic principles (Acts 1:4, 5, 8; 2:41-47; 4:31-33; 5:12-14; 6:1-8; 8:4, 40; 13:19-21, 24; 16:13 ff.; 19:8-10, 20; 28:30-31). Within the framework of these principles, different methods of promulgating the gospel may be effective in different geographical areas and periods of time. Whatever organization of the church's work is necessary to accomplish the task today will be consistent with the precedent of faith and order which is set forth in the New Testament.

(Editor's Note: Dr. Blackwelder originally prepared this article as a paper for the Committee on Christian Unity. A number of other significant study papers have been commissioned by this body, which is now the Commission on Christian Unity.)

A New Approach
To Christian Unity

by
Charles E. Brown

Excerpted from *A New Approach to Christian Unity,* by Charles E. Brown (Anderson, Ind.: Warner Press, Copyright © 1931).

A Time to Remember: TEACHINGS

THE FIRST formal step necessary to get back to the freedom and unity of the apostolic church is to drop all official creeds insofar as they are official and authoritative definitions of denominational belief. The argument is made that it is foolish and absurd to expect to get away from creeds. Every group of people has its unwritten creed; and even every thinking individual has his personal creed. How vain then to think of escaping creeds by laying aside the great historic creeds of the church.

This argument overlooks a serious point. It is admitted that each thoughtful person has a creed of his own. I admit that I have my own creed, in its way, and on some points, as definite as the historic creeds of the churches.

But my personal creed is not a division maker. No other Christian in the world is compelled to sign it in order to have fellowship with me. It is inclusive, and not exclusive. Again, my creed is capable of change. I can sit down with a devout Christian man; and after a few words of prayer we can discuss the Christian faith; and I may arise from that conference with my creed slightly amended. It is doubtless then a better creed; but I did not have to violate a solemn oath to change it a bit; neither did I become a heretic. But many persons are tied up so tightly to official creeds that if they change their own personal creed they have violated a solemn oath. This puts them in a difficult position; for if a man has taken an oath not to believe the truth when he hears it he will take good care not to hear it; but if he should hear it, sometimes he is compelled to believe it in spite of his oath.

Thus it may be seen that there is a world of difference between an official creed, the standard of faith of a denominational corporation, and the private, personal creed of the individual Christian.

The same thing may be said of the unwritten creed of a group of Christians, or a movement. If this creed becomes so hard and narrow that it patently excludes true Christians from fellowship, it is obviously a bad thing. Although even then it can never possess the power to create division that an official creed possesses; because it is always a living and growing thing, capable of responding to the divine guidance of the living Christ in the church. It can broaden with the increase of knowledge.

The apostolic church unquestionably had an unwritten creed. It was the living and growing faith of the church. But this creed never caused division until it narrowed and hardened in the course of centuries into the official, written creed of a human corporation.

Therefore, the first step to Christian unity is to disengage oneself from the historic creeds completely, reverencing them as much as he wishes, believing them as much as he can, but receiving them as mere relics of Christian theological history, and not as standing walls of isolation.

Personally I am an old-fashioned Christian; and I very much suspect that I actually believe the historic creeds much more strongly than the majority of the ministers of the respective demominations; but I would consider it sinful to arm myself with one against my brethren. The will of Christ, the fellowship of all Christians, and the unity of the church are far more precious to me than any human creed ever written.

The second formal step to restore the unity of ancient Christianity is the total abolition of all formal organic denominational divisions among Christian people; not to merge the denominations, but to abolish them is our duty.

This will doubtless sound like anarchy to those dear old souls who have never thought through the inescapable evils of denominationalism. It will shock those who love the historic organizations of men better than the blessed unity of the body of Christ. It will seem revolutionary to the "stand-patters" who spend their time looking back to the good old days of the past. But to all such we would say there is a true place for conservatism in the kingdom of God. Let us look back to the good old days when the church had visible organic unity. Let us remember that the denominations are only a comparatively recent development in the two thousand years history of the church. All signs point to their eventual abolition and the gathering of God's people once again into the blessed peace and unity of the ancient church.

I can well imagine that this doctrine will make a furor among some of those who are great sticklers for order in the church. It would even seem that some people would rather have a dead baby; quiet and orderly—and dignified—than a crying baby that is also quite likely to do things we dislike to see done. I shall be asked how the practical business of the church could ever be carried on in such a system.

To begin with, it is perfectly all right to organize the agencies of the church according to the very best examples of systematic and orderly management of business. We have divine authority for this.

When the Greek-speaking Jews complained because their widows were neglected in the daily ministration, the apostles committed the matter to the church—"and the saying pleased the whole multitude" [i.e. "multitude of the disciples" (see verse 2)] "and they chose Stephen [and six others]" (Acts, sixth chapter). Notice that the church, and not the apostles, chose them. And the Gentile churches appointed a committee to bear their gifts to the poor saints at Jerusalem (1 Cor. 16:3; 2 Cor. 8:19, 23).

This is ample authority for organizing and managing efficiently such bodies as missionary societies, church schools, publishing plants, and the like, for which a denominational organization is usually considered essential.

But one can search in vain for any evidence that the apostolic church was organized as a human corporation in the sense that denominations are organized today.

The apostolic church was organized by the inward urge of the Spirit of God, which led men to undertake the work of preaching and the like, and led the believers to recognize and encourage their call. Where the believers could not sense the existence of the call by the instinct of the indwelling Spirit there was not much danger involved in allowing such a person to exercise himself in some other way till his calling became manifest to the sanctified judgment of the assembly of believers.

The church can only regain her lost visible unity by rallying around our Lord Jesus Christ. In the past there have been cries to rally around this doctrine or that creed, or to rally to this or that battle-cry. Now the call is to come alone to Jesus Christ. "The sceptre shall not depart from Judah, nor a lawgiver from between his feet, until Shiloh come; and unto him shall the gathering of the people be" (Gen. 49:10).

Doctrine is very important; but more important it is to get back to the supreme Person, who is the source of all true doctrine. He has said, "I am the way, the truth, and the life." When all Christendom gets back to him it will be one. There will then be plenty of time to compare and study doctrines, when the clamor of debate has given place to the silence of the humble and earnest pupils in the school of Christ.

God's Clarion Call
by
J. J. M. Nichols-Roy

Excerpted from a booklet entitled, "God's Clarion Call to Christian Unity," published in Los Angeles, Calif., by Mr. Nichols-Roy (n.d.).

THE CALL to Christian unity is as follows:

1. **Keep the Unity of the Spirit.** Every child of God born of the Spirit of God is in the body of Christ, or in the church of God. It is his duty therefore to give diligence to keep this spirit or heart unity. "Walk worthy of the calling wherewith

ye were called, with all lowliness and meekness, with long-suffering, forbearing one another in love, giving diligence to keep the unity of the Spirit in the bond of peace'' (John 10:10, transl. by the writer). We must always remember that God does not want his people to be divided and subdivided, but he wants them to be one for "there is one body and one Spirit, even as also ye were called in one hope of your calling; one Lord, one faith, one baptism, one God and Father of all, who is over all, and through all and in all" (Eph. 4:1-6, ASV). Our Lord said: "And the glory which thou hast given me I have given unto them; that they may be one, even as we are one (John 17:22, ASV). This glory is Christ's own divine nature—his character which produces love, holiness and the force that draws and embraces others of like nature. He said "I have come to give life and to give it more abundantly."

2. **Let unity of faith come by a gradual progress.** The Word says: "Till we all attain unto the unity of the faith, and of the knowledge of the Son of God unto a full grown man, unto the measure of the stature of the fullness of Christ" (Eph. 4:13, ASV). The growth in knowledge comes by a gradual progress. The word *till* in this text and the words *attain unto* indicate this gradual progress. It is evident therefore that there are in the body of Christ or the church of God people of God in different stages of progress in the knowledge of the teachings or doctrines centering in Christ. All the progress is toward the stature of Christ. Everything should be judged or examined by our *soul's relation* with him. No one can claim infallibility or to be a depository of all God's knowledge. Therefore there must be in every heart and mind a great desire to make progress and to get new points and ideas which will lead one to a better knowledge of God's plan and will.

3. **Each one in the body of Christ has the divine privilege of contributing his thoughts and ideas to the body for the building up of that body.** Each one has the liberty to express his views and opinions without fearing other people of God and each one must be anxious and ready and be delighted to

hear what another brother has to say. This idea is expressed by the Holy Spirit through St. Paul in these words: "From whom (Christ) all the body fitly framed and knit together, through that which every joint supplieth, according to the working in due measure of each several part, maketh the increase of the body unto the building up of itself in love" (Eph. 4:16, A.S.V.).

Notice the words, "through that which every joint supplieth." Each member of the body, is, by virtue of his being in that body, given by God a measure of grace and knowledge to impart to others. The condition of the mental and spiritual attitude of the others in the body must be such that each one will feel that blessed liberty without fear of being ostracized directly or indirectly.

4. **Each one must speak the truth in love;** must be gently willing to be criticized and yet feel love for the brethren. Those who criticize also must speak their views in love. "But speaking the truth in love, may grow up in all things into him, who is the head, even Christ" (Eph. 4:15, ASV). Our minds and hearts must always be guided by the thoughts and feelings of our Lord. "The peace of God, which passeth all understanding, shall guard your hearts and your thoughts in Christ Jesus" (Phil. 4:7).

The Unity
Of the Spirit
by
Harold L. Phillips

Excerpted from *Vital Christianity,* October 4, 1964.

A Time to Remember: TEACHINGS

THIS EDITORIAL takes the stance that God wills for his People (the church of the living God) a fellowship type of unity which the Holy Spirit himself creates among the followers of Christ. This is the type of unity for which Christ prayed. This is the type of unity God gives to those who yearn for it.

Paul urged the Ephesian Christians and all others to whom this early Christian epistle was sent "to preserve the unity of the Spirit in the bond of peace" (Eph. 4:3, NAS). This admonition likewise confronts the church in our time with imperatives of faith and action.

Careful reading of this passage would suggest that Paul was evidently writing about a unity which already existed, a present reality rather than a pious or distant hope. He definitely was not saying, "Brethren, if you ever figure out some way to achieve unity, be sure to hang onto it once you have managed it."

This phrase in Ephesians about "the unity of the Spirit" might well be paraphrased, "the unity which the Spirit creates." It is the unity of vine and branches, the unity of head and body, the unity of members in one body, the unity of a King and his Kingdom.

In essence the church is the fellowship of Christian believers who are bound together by common participation in the grace of God, the guidance of the Spirit, and the gifts and promises of God to his People. Christian believers live "in Christ" and it is from this realtionship that their deepest unity springs.

In a sense, then, the unity God wills for his People is first of all a "spiritual" rather than an institutional, doctrinal, or mechanical unity. This is not to say that ways of working together are unimportant or that matters of doctrine are of no concern. It is simply putting first things first. It is putting the priority where the New Testament puts the priority. God wants an "authentic" rather than a contrived unity.

Personal and vital experience of Christ is foundational, then, to the unity that God wills. This is unity with a vertical as well as a horizontal dimension. This is unity created by

Christ rather than man, a unity *in him*. In Christ and through the Holy Spirit God's people are one—now.

Before the church is anything else, it is the body of Christ, and when it ceases to be this it is no longer the church but a man-made institution. When the church at Corinth was threatened with division because Christians began to look to human leaders ahead of Christ, Paul reminded them, "Now you are Christ's body, and individually members of it" (1 Cor. 12:27, NAS).

The intention here is not to disparage the necessity of having organization in the church or institutional manifestations of the work of the church, but rather to establish priorities, to put the unity emphasis today in the same place where the New Testament puts it.

As one commentator has stated so aptly, "The New Testament shows a singular disregard for the church in its organizational and institutional aspects." That this is so will become evident to anyone who bothers to read it with care.

The modern ecumenical movement stands at a point of danger here and none are more aware of it than some leaders already prominent in that movement. They sense the possibility that the grand ecumenical ideal might become institutionalized and that many church leaders might tend to settle for an organizational structure as being the achievement of Christian unity.

Others insist that the experimental approach, the fellowship approach, the New Testament approach, to Christian unity is the real need of the hour. This is the kind of unity that we can dare say God wills. This by no means rules out serious efforts to find ways of working together fruitfully and to find ways to express more adequately the unity that already exists.

Right at this point we must be prepared for at least some measure of disillusionment if we envision that by some sudden and almost magic means all the barriers between denominations are going to drop away. Denominational differences are more stubbornly entrenched than that.

Also, real unity, being relational in character, can be

enhanced only where a spirit of repentance exists and when the desire for unity becomes greater than the will to preserve cherished traditional differences. Where there is unwillingness to permit life to be transformed by the action of the Holy Spirit, significant unity cannot come.

"We Favor Outlawing War"

Passed by the General Ministerial Assembly of the Church of God, June 22, 1928.

WHEREAS, it is an undoubted fact that warfare has caused untold misery and suffering to the human race, and

WHEREAS, war as a method of settling international disputes is contrary to the principles and teachings of Jesus, and

WHEREAS, it is a growing sentiment among Christians everywhere that war should be outlawed and abolished from the face of the earth as an enemy of the progress of the human race and a detriment to the propagation of the Christian religion, therefore

BE IT RESOLVED, that we, the General Ministerial Assembly of the Church of God convened in session June 22, 1928, hereby declare ourselves in favor of every effort being put forward by our government and the governments of other nations, and the various leagues that are organized to propagate the principles of peace, which have for their aim the outlawry of war.

Resolution on War

Passed by the General Ministerial Assembly of the Church of God, June 23, 1932.

IN ACCORDANCE with the Pact of Paris, otherwise known as the Kellogg Pact, signed at Paris, August 27, 1928, whereby 56 nations solemnly denounced war as an instrument of national policy and agreed to settle all disputes or conflicts by pacific means, we make the following declaration:

> War is unchristian, futile and suicidal, and we denounce completely the whole war system. We will never again sanction or participate in any war. We will not use our pulpits or classrooms as recruiting stations. We set ourselves to educate and lead youth in the principle and practice of goodwill, justice, understanding, brotherhood, and peace. We will not give our financial or moral support to any war. We will seek security and justice by pacific means.

"A Vigorous Objection"

Passed by the General Ministerial Assembly of the Church of God, June 18, 1947.

WHEREAS this suffering and battered world even yet staggers under the shock of wars past, present, and future; and

WHEREAS the only bright rays of hope appear in the valiant efforts of relief of hunger and suffering abroad and in the aid given toward achieving material and spiritual reconstruction; and

WHEREAS we as a religious body have participated in such efforts and expect to continue to do so to the extent of our abilities; but

WHEREAS there is a vigorous campaign for conscripting the youth of our churches and nation for compulsory peacetime military training; and

WHEREAS the alleged benefits of such training are nullified by exposure to immoral influences coincident with the military life; and

WHEREAS the use of atomic warfare techniques would nullify the use of traditional armed forces; and

WHEREAS such preparation for war is no guarantee of peace, but, rather, creates an atmosphere which crystallizes the threat of war into the actuality; and

WHEREAS education for peacetime pursuits for uplifting mankind would be replaced by education for death and destruction; and

WHEREAS the need of our day is the erasure of malice, suspicion, and misunderstanding; and for the promotion of brotherhood, mutual trust, and the ministry of healing; and

WHEREAS the democratic processes of our government would be threatened by further growth of the military establishment; therefore

BE IT RESOLVED that the General Ministerial Assembly of the Church of God, assembled at Anderson, Indiana, June 18, 1947, commend the leaders of our nation for the splendid work of relief and rehabilitation which they have directed; but

BE IT FURTHER RESOLVED that we register vigorous objection to any plan for peacetime conscription of youth for military training; and

BE IT FURTHER RESOLVED that the secretary of this Assembly be instructed to send a copy of this resolution to the President of the United States, to the presiding officers of both houses of Congress, and to their respective military affairs committees, and to the Secretary of War.

Statement of Conviction

Passed by the General Assembly of the Church of God, June 14, 1966.

LIKE ALL true Americans, we as members of the General Assembly of the Church of God meeting in regular session in Anderson, Indiana, this sixteenth day of June, 1966, view with deep concern the escalating military involvement and the conscription of our youth for military service. We believe that war represents our moral failures. We abhor the causes that lead to war. We stand by the teaching and example of our Lord who taught us and showed us the way of radical, sacrificial love.

We are thankful to God that we live in a land of basic freedoms whose law makes provision for alternative service by those "who, by reason of religious training and belief, are conscientiously opposed to participation in war in any form." We encourage our young men who conscientiously object to war to engage in such civilian work which contributes "to the maintenance of the national health, safety or interest."

We respect the right of each person to arrive at his own convictions. We believe in the principle of freedom of worship and freedom of conscience. We respect the rights of the individual conscience within our fellowship. We have never set up an authoritative creed. Instead, we accept the entire New Testament as our rule of faith and practice, and we seek to lead every member of our fellowship to full comprehension and full acceptance of the Spirit of Christ as the guide for all conduct. What we seek for ourselves we seek for every citizen of our land—the right of individual conscience which no governmental authority can abrogate or violate. We do not condemn or reject that person who differs with our position or participates in war. We shall seek to follow such persons with a ministry of help and guidance, but this is never to be construed as approval of war.

We fervently pray for the leaders of our nation and of other nations, many of whom we believe to be sincerely striving for peace. We pray that efforts by negotiation among countries, through the United Nations, and every possible channel may succeed in bringing peace to our troubled world. Let this statement of conviction be construed by any and all to mean that we fully support young men of the Church of God who sincerely and conscientiously are opposed to participation in military service. We encourage them to seek the constructive alternatives intended to bring health, healing, and understanding, and which serve the highest interests of our beloved country and of the whole world.

Between Pacifism
And Nationalism

by
Hollis S. Pistole

THE CHURCH OF GOD cannot readily be identified as one of the historic "peace churches" in the manner of the Quakers, Mennonites, and Brethren. However, if one regards seriously the official statements and resolutions on war and peace as an indication of the church's convictions, there is ample reason for referring to it as a "peace church."

Unlike the historic peace churches, the Church of God has not placed a studied and continuous emphasis on the issues of war and peace. Early statements in the *Gospel Trumpet* were in response to questions from readers. Other announcements either in the *Gospel Trumpet* or other church publications were related to immediate needs such as the draft in World War I. These were designed to inform the constituency of the rights of those persons seeking a non-military role as opposed to regular service with the armed forces. Subsequent resolutions placed before the ministerial assemblies were usually the work of small committees dealing with specific concerns. Nor has there been any on-going emphasis on peace education in the church through the years.

The Church of God has not espoused a strong pacifist position and demanded that this be binding on all. Rather, it has recognized that each Christian has a right to his or her own conviction on this issue. A young person can serve in good faith either in the military or in alternative service as a conscientious objector. It is apparent that in general only a few Church of God young people have requested and re-

201 (441)

ceived non-combat positions and served as medical attendants or chaplain assistants.

The issue of "thou shalt not kill" has come under serious scrutiny by church leaders. Is this a prohibition against murder specifically or against the taking of life in any manner for whatever reason? Most holiness churches have tended to interpret the commandment on the first basis and thus have permitted participation by Christians in what might be termed "just wars." It has been deemed permissible for Christians to resist the "aggressor" and to deter the "evil force." Holiness churches generally have supported the United States in its several military engagements. They have seen Church and State as both ordained by God, but with different functions. This has had the effect of tempering the pacifist position by the assumption that the State is also God's instrument and is entitled to our obedience. Historic peace churches have not been sympathetic to this attitude toward the State and have felt that Christians who give such allegiance to the State are compromising.

The Church of God has found itself somewhere between these two positions of a total commitment to pacifism and what often appears to be a capitulation to the State and compulsory military service. It has not been felt that loyalty to God and country are necessarily in conflict. Attention has been called to the fact that this nation provides by law for the right of alternative service for the conscientious objector. The Church of God has treasured this as a high liberty for citizens, even though it has not insisted that such conscientious objection necessarily become a standard for the church.

Following the advent of the Vietnam War in the 1960s, two groups have functioned to aid young men in the Church of God in thinking about participation in military service. The first group is the Social Concerns Commission which was established in 1964 by the Executive Council of the Church of God. One of the several assignments of this Commission is in the area of war and peace. The other force for peace education in the church is the Church of God Peace Fellowship. This is a totally voluntary group of interested persons independent of national church structures which has sought through its modest publications and conferences to keep the cause of peace before the church. This group goes back to the work of the late Dean Russell Olt of Anderson College and Dr. Mack Caldwell of Warner Pacific College and more recently of Warner Southern College.

Perhaps the most important thing about the concern for peace is the fact that the Church of God has from its earliest days expressed a deep concern for the non-violent approach to the settling of issues. Surely there are no stronger statements against war to be found among the historic peace churches than those stated by the General Ministerial Assembly in its 1928 and 1932 resolutions.

As we move toward our centennial observance it is to be hoped that this dimension of our church heritage may be renewed in ways that will speak meaningfully to our youth in generations to come.

The Ultimate Promise Of Our Lord
by
Lillie S. McCutcheon

Excerpted from *Dynamics of the Faith,* ed. by Gene Miller et. al. (Houston, Tex.: Gulf-Coast Bible College, 1972).

THE MOST treasured prophecy for the church is the promise of the Lord, "I will come again, and receive you unto myself; that where I am, there ye may be also" (John 14:3). Christ's prophecies concerning Jerusalem's destruction came to pass in the generation of Jews who cried, " . . . His blood be on us, and on our children" (Matt. 27:25). False christs have come and gone in every generation. "For many shall come in my name, saying, I am Christ; and shall deceive many" (Matt. 24:5). The great apostasy transpired through the Dark Ages.

The gospel is gradually preached to all nations and judgment has fallen on nations who reject Christ. "And this gospel of the kingdom shall be preached in all the world for a witness unto all nations; and then shall the end come" (Matt. 24:14).

The God who prepared the world for the first coming of his Son now makes world preparations for the second advent. Truly the Lord said, "But of that day and hour knoweth no man, no, not the angels of heaven, but my Father only" (Matt. 24:36). The manner of Christ's coming is told by angels, " . . . this same Jesus, which is taken up from you into heaven, shall so come in like manner as ye have seen him go into heaven" (Acts 1:11). The herald of his coming is the sounding of a trumpet "for the Lord himself shall descend from heaven with a shout, with the voice of the archangel, and with the trump of God" (1 Thess. 4:16).

The purposes of Christ's coming are:

(1) **To resurrect the dead.** "Marvel not at this: for the hour is coming, in the which all that are in the graves shall hear his voice, And shall come forth; they that have done good unto the resurrection of life; and they that have done evil, unto the resurrection of damnation" (John 5:28-29);

(2) **The consummation of the age and destruction of the earth.** "But the day of the Lord will come as a thief in the night; in the which the heavens shall pass away with a great noise, and the elements shall melt with fervent heat, the earth also and the works that are therein shall be burned up" (2 Peter 3:10);

(3) **To bring judgment.** " . . . Jesus Christ who shall judge the quick and the dead at his appearing . . ." (2 Tim. 4:1);

(4) **To grant rewards.** "For the Son of man shall come in the glory of his Father with his angels: and then he shall reward every man according to his works" (Matt. 16:27);

(5) **To deliver up the kingdom.** "Then cometh the end, when he shall have delivered up the kingdom to God, even the Father . . ." (1 Cor. 15:24);

(6) **To claim his bride, the church.** " . . . for the marriage of the Lamb is come, and his wife hath made herself ready" (Rev. 19:7);

(7) **The final doom of the enemies of the church.** "And the devil that deceived them was cast into the lake of fire and brimstone, where the beast and the false prophet are . . . and whosoever was not found written in the book of life was cast into the lake of fire" (Rev. 20:10-15).

John climaxes the prophecies of the church with a beautiful description of her heavenly home. He makes a striking contrast with the Eden in Genesis compared with the paradise of God in the new heaven and new earth. "Nevertheless we, according to his promise, look for new heavens and a new earth, wherein dwelleth righteousness" (2 Peter 3:13). Eden had its sin, tears, tempter, pain, forbidden tree, and death. In the New Jerusalem none of these shall ever enter. The tree of life perpetually bears fruit and the redeemed of all ages behold God's face forever. The triumphant praises of a church victorious shall echo forever in a world without end.

INDEX

MAJOR TOPICS

D. S. Warner
His son, Sidney
and wife, Frances
ca. 1894

Joseph C. Fisher

Charles W. Naylor

D. Otis Teasley
and Family

Barney E. Warren
1901

Herbert M. Riggle

A. T. Rowe

Charles E. Byers

Kenneth F. Hall

EDITORS OF
GOSPEL TRUMPET—VITAL CHRISTIANITY

D. S. Warner
1880-1895

E. E. Byrum
1895-1916

F. G. Smith
1916-1930

C. E. Brown
1930-1951

Arlo F. Newell
1977-

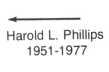

Harold L. Phillips
1951-1977

212 (452)

DEANS OF
ANDERSON SCHOOL OF THEOLOGY

Earl L. Martin
1950-1953

Adam W. Miller
1953-1962

Gene W. Newberry
1962-1974

Barry L. Callen
1974-

Gospel Trumpet Editorial Staff
1956

Warner Press Editorial Staff
1977

'CHRISTIAN BROTHERHOOD HOUR' SPEAKERS

W. Dale Oldham
1947-1968

R. Eugene Sterner
1968-1977

James E. Massey
1977-

Fidel Zamorano
(CBH-Spanish) 1965-

EXECUTIVE COUNCIL

1977 Session

| W. E. Reed | Edward L. Foggs |
| Executive Secretary | Assoc. Exec. Secretary |

216 (456)